SIX GOOD INNINGS

SIX GOOD INNINGS

How One Small Town Became a
LITTLE LEAGUE GIANT

MARK KREIDLER

HARPER

An Imprint of HarperCollins*Publishers*

www.harpercollins.com

HarperCollins books may be purchased for educational, business, or sales promotional use. For information, please write: Special Markets Department, HarperCollins Publishers, 10 East 53rd Street, New York, NY 10022.

FIRST EDITION

Title page photograph of 2007 Toms River American All-Stars courtesy of Vinny Ignatowicz.

Designed by William Ruoto

Library of Congress Cataloging-in-Publication Data is available upon request.

ISBN: 978-0-06-147357-9

08 09 10 11 12   ID/RRD   10 9 8 7 6 5 4 3 2 1

To Patric and Ryan, for every day

And again to Colleen,
With love and a table at Alfonso's

**"It breaks your heart.
It is designed to break your heart."**

—A. Bartlett Giamatti, former commissioner of
Major League Baseball, *A Great and Glorious Game*

CONTENTS

PROLOGUE

I T   W A S   A L L   T H E R E   I N   the sound. Chris didn't need to look. Every Little League kid who could hit his weight knew what the different bats sounded like when they met a baseball just so, and this one had an unmistakable tone and quality to it. It was impossible to confuse it with anything else, this kind of weird thunk; a wood bat wouldn't in a million years produce that sound, and ordinary metal or aluminum models don't quite replicate it, tending more toward a resounding, echoing ping that can be heard all over a baseball complex. No, this was the noise—really, the just-barely-a-noise—that only a top-of-the-line, composite material bat could create, and only when a pitch had been crushed, hit dead-solid perfect. In this case, a $200 DeMarini F3 had been swung to a square meeting with a Little League–approved, five-ounce, three-dollar baseball, and what came out, sonically, was that thunk. It was a sound thickened and flattened by the swampy Jersey Shore humidity, and it indicated serious travel. That ball was going places.

And standing there, taking in the moment, Chris Gulla didn't have to ask. It wasn't his first home run, after all. He had smacked his share as a hitter, and he had given up a few as a pitcher, and in Toms River that was just the way of life by age 12. It came with being great and competing against the best. As a hitter, you needed to be able to drive a ball at least 200 feet anytime an opposing pitcher made a mistake and left one there for you right over the strike zone, if you had the slightest design on success or even inclusion among the elite. Chris, his face freckled and cherubic but his body already growth-spurting its way toward a looming adolescence, was getting there. He was strong enough to belt a home run off any pitcher's gaffe—he'd already done it once today—and, on the mound, he was a good enough pitcher, when healthy, to avoid such a fate most of the time. He was in every important respect an All-Star, which is to say he was a small god. More than that, he was a returning All-Star, a once-triumphant 11-year-old now turned 12, part of a Toms River tradition that featured some of the most audacious winning in the history of the sport. He lived in a place where athletic excellence by sixth grade wasn't so much demanded as simply assumed, and both baseball smarts and outsized ambition were a given.

And just this instant, to be specific, Chris was part of a team that had already decided on its final destination in the summer of 2007: Williamsport, Pennsylvania. Anything short of a place at the Little League World Series, an event that Toms River had by then come to claim almost as a birthright, would go down on the books as a flat failure. Chris's teammates wanted it all. They were going to bring the glory back to the town, back to the place that had first captured it more than a decade ago, and they knew they could do it. Given what they had accomplished just one summer before, it was an easy conclusion to reach. They were gifted and experienced. They could hit home runs to win games. They could beat teams with their smarts, and with their uncanny ability to avoid the kinds of pitfalls that routinely doomed other rosters full of fifth-, sixth- and seventh-graders. They could play so well, so composed that they seemed older than they actually were. They were winners, born of a winning attitude.

"There is," one player said, "no such thing as losing here."

History said so. Thunk after thunk after thunk.

So Chris knew the sound, and he knew right away that the impact could be major. His pulse quickened at the thought that the ball was going out. Home runs were the lifeblood of the great All-Star teams; if homers weren't a common occurrence by now in your games over at Toms River Little League's sprawling, eight-field, million-dollar complex along Mapletree Road, something was dreadfully wrong. And the first indication that a ball was gone, before anyone really saw it jump off the bat or tried to figure the trajectory, before the moms and dads looked up to see the outfielders backtracking and the fielders themselves looking over their shoulders helplessly to the area beyond the fence—the first indication was usually in the sound. The sound pronounced a winner.

John Puleo heard it. He was watching the whole thing unfold. For the better part of two summers, John had been guiding this group of kids to a specific time, and he now realized that a decisive moment might be upon them. He was 48 years old, the brother of a former Major Leaguer, the father of one of the best players on the Toms River team. He was a coach whose relentlessly upbeat approach and almost slavish dedication to the routines and extremes of practice had delivered Toms River both district and section championships in 2006, and had set the level of expectation for these boys as 12-year-olds. It is only when you're 12 that the Little League World Series becomes more than a theoretical possibility, becomes a thing that can actually be attained. When you're 12, you can go to the Show. And when you are 12 in Toms River, that is more than a mere delicious thought. Toms River knows firsthand that Williamsport could be both a dream *and* a reality.

To be sure, John Puleo had bought into the dream right alongside the kids. He had seen everything from 2006, seen what this team was capable of and the ways the boys seemed constantly to cheat defeat and move on. He had gone to extraordinary lengths to ensure that the '06 group didn't fall apart, that it stayed together practicing and thriving through the coldest winter months, with a sense of purpose and some respect for its forebears. The team would be together at least long enough for this push toward the World Series, the chance to join the other legendary rosters from the town—the ones who had gone to Williamsport and shone so brightly. It had happened here before, to local kids who became national heroes. Their names were painted onto signs that hung on walls and above baseball buildings in town, the names of the kids who played for the winning Toms River teams of the past. John's players wanted their names on the wall, and so John wanted it—for his players, for his Little League, for his son and himself, all of it. There was no pretending otherwise. Around the Shore, you never played coy when it came to baseball. You went for it.

And they were all aware of that, by July 2007. By then, after all they had been through together, the Toms River kids were dialed in to everything that was going on, right down to the moment of the pitch and the swing of the bat. They were keeping track of almost everything, filtering all of it through the context of their hopes. By the time of this particular moment, almost all of them had already formed their opinions about Coach John's game strategies, debating silently and among themselves whether the coach had the right idea about how to attack this particular opponent. It didn't matter now. The game was already on. The thing was in play.

It was in play, and they all heard that sound, the thunk. Most of them looked up, knowing the ball was jumping off the bat. Chris Gulla reflexively reached with his left hand to feel his sore right arm. Out in the bleachers beyond right-center field, Diane Puleo, John's wife, saw the path of the ball and quietly closed the cell phone with which she had been trying to call her husband on the field. From the dugout, John walked fully into the haze and squinted straight up into a tremendously bright sun, trying to track the flight of the hit. It was a great, high sky. The heat was radiating, almost pulsing through the humid air; you could soak your shirt just standing there. All in all, baseball players would call it great hitting weather.

So it was. The ball went up, taking off like a bottle

rocket. It almost lacked an arc, it had been hit so hard. Chris was right about one thing: You didn't need to look. It was a little bit beautiful, really. And John Puleo squinted up, and he considered everything, and he wondered what magnitude of mistake he'd just made, and whether his team would survive it.

CHAPTER 1

VIEW FROM ON HIGH

As their coach approached the practice field, having pulled his black-and-gray Chevy Suburban as close as possible to the baseball diamond, the players could see that he was toting something out of the ordinary. By now, the boys of John Puleo's Toms River American Little League team were accustomed to seeing him show up at the league's Mapletree Road complex in possession of the usual baseball workout gear: buckets of balls, batting tees, hitting nets, a team bag full of batting helmets, weighted swing donuts, the extra bats that no one used anymore because each kid by now either had his own high-end model or borrowed one from a teammate. It was all fairly standard stuff. Having played for 56 straight days the summer before, the guys all knew the drill: help Coach John unload the equipment; put it to serious use for three-plus hours, even though he told their parents they'd be done in two; load it up again when the workout was over. Sometimes they did it twice in a day.

But this afternoon was different. Today, a weekday smack in the middle of June, wasn't just any other practice day; it was the first workout for the All-Stars of 2007, who, without so much as playing a game, had already been identified as the team to beat. And John had something else in mind.

The faces around him were familiar. It was basically the same group of players that had captured the district title, New Jersey Little League District 18, in a stunning break-through in 2006, when the boys competed together as 11-year-olds. That had been, in almost every respect, the best baseball summer of their lives, a little unexpected and a lot glorious, and when Toms River American went on to win the section title and finish third in the state of New Jersey, it seemed as though a story line and a sound track already had been laid down for the looming summer of 2007. In '07 the boys would be 12—or at least "baseball 12," mean-ing that none of them had become a teenager before May 1. In truth, a couple of them were already 13 by the time the first practice rolled around—and such was to be the case for almost every team Toms River American would face, be-cause that's how the rules were drawn. In fact, among evenly matched opponents, especially at the higher levels of the tournaments—the state and regional competitions and the holy grail of Williamsport itself—winning or losing could, and often did, come down to how many 13s were out there masquerading as 12s, and whose kids had grown the most since last year. No one who had ever seen a kid hit puberty would argue the point.

Scotty Ringel was 13, and he looked it. A year ago, Scotty had been one of Toms River's unquestioned leaders:

a pitcher who at times appeared almost untouchable; a hitter who could drive a ball on a straight line over the fence. He was a beast. Then, to the encouragement of all concerned, the boy had proceeded to grow to his teenage dimensions. Lank and brown-haired, Scotty had sinewy arms and stilt legs, and, looking from the outside in, one might be tempted to conclude that he had grown too much, too quickly to stay coordinated, as he reached steadily toward 5 feet 8 inches. Instead, Scotty had slipped into his new frame with surprising gracefulness. He might get tied up on a dance floor, but when it came to sports he had retained almost all of his coordination and his sense of timing, which was so critical to his ability to hit a baseball. Scotty was a multisport athlete, in contrast to many of the Toms River kids who focused exclusively on baseball. The extensive time he had put in as an elite-level basketball and soccer player was paying off here on the diamond: he was both sure-handed and sure-footed, and even with his new, larger frame he could comfortably lower his center of gravity toward the grass as he levered himself into position to field a ground ball. He had great flexibility, and he could still move quickly. He could run the bases and hit with power. He was, absolutely, a player John and the Toms River Americans knew they could count on.

But Scotty was a leader almost exclusively in deed. He was the kind of kid who would listen to his teammates in the dugout laughing and joking, smile to himself and not really join in or even speak a word. He left the chatter to guys like Vinny Ignatowicz and Andrew Hourigan, players who were more than happy to fill the rare quiet moment in a dugout with the sound of their voices. Scotty didn't mind the noise; in fact, he loved the baseball tradition of yapping and encouraging one another in between every pitch. But it wasn't his way. He processed almost every emotion internally; even his father, Scott, often wouldn't see or hear how his son felt about things until hours or days after a game, and even then only in a clipped sentence or a small observation that revealed Scotty's inner thoughts.

Scotty didn't fluster easily, and he didn't cheerlead. It wasn't until he crossed onto the field that he was transformed into a player who could inspire his teammates by the sheer dint of how hard he worked and how good he was at the game. Like Johnny Puleo, the coach's son, Scotty played with a passion and an intensity that was impossible not to recognize. His teammates fed off that—sometimes it even seemed as if they were waiting for Scotty to come out there and take care of things for them—and Scotty in turn accepted his responsibility. He had no qualms about being thought of as a critical component in Toms River's success, because that's how he thought of himself. In that sense, he and Johnny Puleo were kindred spirits. They wanted the action. They didn't mind the pressure. Last summer, when things all went so perfectly, a leader is exactly what Scotty had been, and then he had gone and grown another several inches, and he certainly looked like a player who was bound again to lead. Scotty was tall and lean, but above all strong. John, sizing up his roster, figured that Scotty might well need those broad shoulders.

As he stood at the field watching Coach John approach the players, Scotty felt that he had already come to understand the competitive terrain Toms River would be covering this year. He knew what last year's third-place finish at the state tournament meant: he and his mates were now the team to beat. Everybody—everybody—would be gunning for them. It wasn't like in years past, when Toms River had the history but local rival Jackson, with its great pitching and its uncanny ability to win close games, kept pulling down all the titles. Now it was Scotty and his guys who were the defending champs, and now there were no longer any easy games. Toms River had slipped past a few unsuspecting opponents last summer, perhaps because those teams were too busy worrying about Jackson. That wasn't going to happen this time around—and Scotty was ready for that.

Johnny was ready, too. Wiry, with dark hair and eyes, the coach's son was possessed of a broad smile that he kept hidden most of the time he was on the baseball field. There, he gravitated toward the more serious ballplayer look, one that often featured black eyeshade smudged in a line across each cheekbone, indicating a willingness to play the game for keeps, warrior-style. Johnny had waited months for the All-Star competition that he considered the truly good stuff of the year. He already had shaken off the doldrums that inevitably accompanied the Little League's regular season, the vast expanse of time from February to June when he and the other returning All-Stars were scattered among Toms River American Little League's teams: a few to the Red Sox, a few to the White Sox, Rangers, and so on. The regular season bore almost no connection to All-Stars. The best athletes played for whatever team drafted them (or, in Johnny's case, the Red Sox team that his father had agreed to coach), in an effort to give all Little League teams a chance at being equally competitive. It wasn't until the season neared its end that the league's coaches and managers got together to pick the All-Star rosters in each age group, the adults bringing forward the names of the players they viewed as the elite.

The regular season was a series of games among Toms River Little League's teams in both National and American divisions. They were fun games to play, with none of the pressure that accompanied the All-Star process, where every pitch carried the potential of either victory or elimination. But it was tempting during those long weeks of the regular season, playing as part of less talented rosters that by their nature incorporated younger and weaker players, to relax and fall into the recreation-ball aspect of Little League, the sort of everyone-plays, no-score-matters mantra that the organization often liked to project as its image. In April and May, even in a competitive town like Toms River, it was difficult not to lie back and focus on the snow cone or hot dog that would be waiting afterward, and to put less stock in the games themselves. If you were strictly out there for fun, it was your time of year.

But, of course, no returning All-Star would lie back like that. If you understood what you were doing, then you understood that the regular season was the time to work on a new pitch, to tinker with your batting stance. The games might not matter, but the timeline did. If you were an All-Star, then the road through the regular season actually led straight to June and July, and if you spent April and May mostly goofing off, it might tell when it came time to show your best stuff in All-Star play. In Scotty's mind, there was no excuse for losing the edge—and, at any rate, Scotty was incapable of relaxed baseball. He possessed a pronounced inability to take it easy when it came to sports—an all-or-nothing proposition as an athlete, one who was willing to work himself beyond exhaustion to improve his game by a percent. It was, in so many ways, what made him the perfect sort of player to carry on the Toms River tradition.

SCOTTY STOOD WITH HIS TEAMMATES on the practice field, watching Coach John walk over, and he already knew what to expect: It was going to be a brutal session. John Puleo was perhaps the most upbeat, encouraging Little League coach in Toms River, but when it came to practice and preparation he was not going to see his team outworked by anybody along the Jersey Shore—and after last summer's success there was a zero percent chance that the coach would alter his approach to getting ready for All-Star competition. The Toms River players of 2006 had logged hours, swings, throws and miles that would be unthinkable in most towns, and they had won big doing it. What in theory sounded aggressive to the point of unhealthy—who in his right mind would work a group of 11-year-olds for hours a day, for 56 days straight?—had in reality played out to a surpassing result. The plan yielded so many victories and hoisting of championship banners that it became impossible to argue against it. The boys might well have won the games they did on a lighter schedule, but that was just a guess. What was fact was that they won the way they did, with no days off, and now they already knew that they could count on this summer being more of the same.

Looking the boys over, John knew what he had: a returning championship team. John and his coaches—Paul Fabricatore and Jerry Volk, along with Scott Ringel, Scotty's father—wanted to tinker as little as possible with last year's roster, and with good reason. It wasn't that the collection of talent was world class, although "American," as the team often referred to itself, certainly had talent. Scotty had thrown more than 20 consecutive innings without giving up an earned run during the 2006 All-Star tournaments. Puleo's son Johnny was a steadily improving shortstop who had really made strides as a top-level pitcher during the regular season, playing for John's Red Sox entry in Toms River Little League. Quintin Garvin, another Red Sox player, was a wonderful if volcanic talent, by some accounts the best center-fielder in the state at his age. If he could get out of his own way and stop beating himself up over every little mistake, Quintin might well outshine everyone on the field. Pauly Schifilliti was a multitool guy, and he might be a surprising weapon as a pitcher because of his signature knuckle-curveball. Andrew Hourigan, naturally gifted in virtually every sport he attempted, played baseball with an almost effortless grace, and he had speed and the ability to pitch, too. And there was the quintessential late bloomer, Vinny Ignatowicz, a reserve on the 2006 team who suddenly was hitting shots over fences and easily running down fly balls in the outfield.

They were all going to be huge. They all had the potential to do something magnificent out there over the next eight weeks. There was talent, absolutely.

Still, John knew, the truly great teams were always more than the sums of their talent, and that had been true for John's squad the summer before. That team had succeeded in part because of its wonderful chemistry, which almost organically produced its own level of expectation. It showed in the way the guys got along, how they carried themselves, and the work they were so willing to put in, all in the hopes of making something great happen together. The parents meshed, which was always so critical in putting together a winning youth team. No one ever acted like his kid was the reason the team was winning; the Toms River parents were too baseball savvy for that, and their team-first attitude appeared to trickle down to the players themselves. And everyone was up for the adventure itself: the hours, the drives, the weather. What was required was very nearly a complete sacrifice of the summer, and in 2006 the players, the coaches and the families made the sacrifice happily, almost easily. Something clicked there—John couldn't always describe it, but he had felt it while it was happening—and it had to do with the combination of talent and personality, just the right amount of both. He was in no hurry to monkey with any of that.

These boys were growing up in a baseball town, in a part of the world that took the sport seriously, surrounded by adults with a love of the game and a passion for teaching it, amid the general expectation of winning and then winning some more. That passion sometimes bled into mania; the mania occasionally spilled over to extremes. The pressure on 12-year-olds to perform as if they were already elite-level talents was, by acclaim, enormous. But to hear people in Toms River tell it, the extremes were often a necessary component of the success, seldom worth apologizing for. And at the heart of it all was the game, and the system. The kids were learning and having a good time and winning. They saw no downside at all.

Now, here on the first day of their most important summer together, John knew exactly how he wanted to greet the boys, and the effect that he wanted his greeting to create. As he drew closer to the field, striding purposefully toward it, he summoned the players to the pitcher's mound, telling them to put down the baseballs and stop their warm-up throws. He wanted them, all 13 of the Americans, to form a circle around him, and after they did, he waited until they quieted down and were looking at him expectantly.

John unfolded the giant photograph and spread it out for everyone to see.

"This is where we want to go," the coach said simply.

When Vinny looked down on the infield grass, he saw, rolled open to its poster-size dimension, a color aerial shot of Williamsport, Pennsylvania. To get there from Toms River, it took about five hours in a car and a whole bunch of baseball victories at precisely the right moment. Vinny and Pauly stood and looked down at the photo, and they could easily spot the Little League International Headquarters, the center of the most extensive and popular youth sports organization in the world. If you knew anything at all about the place, which the Toms River kids and their parents certainly did, then you could trace the outline of Howard J. Lamade Stadium, the field upon which the World Series championship game was to be played in August, 10 weeks from now. That game would draw a sitting and standing crowd of around 40,000 people, and it would be broadcast to millions more via national television, with the ABC network carrying the ESPN production. Kids and their parents all around the world would tune in to watch.

Williamsport was, without a doubt, the great stage in the self-obsessed universe of youth baseball. And John had it right: It was where Toms River—individually, collectively and as a community of baseball-first families—wanted to go.

Vinny had been dreaming about Williamsport for months. The regular Little League season for him, playing on an Angels team that won just a handful of games, had amounted to one overlong tune-up for All-Star play. Vinny hadn't found it easy to return to the regular season in 2007, even though, as one of the Angels' best players, he got to spend a fair amount of his time smacking line drives and home runs. There was always the letdown factor for the better kids, as they found themselves stuck back on the age-group merry-go-round, with sixth- and seventh-graders trying to figure out how to play alongside fourth- or fifth-grade teammates. Vinny's team hadn't been any good—the wrong combination of returning players and new guys. It happened to most of the teams every year. Coach John's Red Sox had seemed to reload from the year before, but for everyone else, it was the usual scramble.

Beneath the blond hair, blue-gray eyes and rapid-joking demeanor that gave him the appearance of a Jersey Shore vacationer as much as anything else, Vinny in his heart had never stopped being a member of the district and sectional champion All-Star squad from the summer before. It was so much more than just being on a good team; there was a connection. These guys, as a group, were hot. They could play, all of them. They knew how to win. There were no weak links. You didn't have to waste your time with some kid whose mom or dad had forced him into a uniform; these were the guys who really wanted to be out there. Vinny got through the regular season fine, even enjoyed some of it. But he couldn't wait for June, because June meant the good stuff. The boy had long ago lost the ability to fake humility or hide his ambition. He was a Toms River All-Star, and he was ready for the full experience this time around.

And there it was, on the ground in front of him: a photo that represented precisely the experience he wanted, as if Coach John had read his mind. This was the destination that Vinny and his teammates had already been talking about. They weren't afraid to consider going to the World Series. In fact, they couldn't help but do so. It was hard to live in Toms River and not at least entertain the possibility that your team would be the next Little League squad to bring home the glory.

The photo lay there, rolled out, the grass forming a carpet underneath it. The hot sun was still hanging high in the sky. Vinny already knew that before practice was over, he'd feel like he was standing in a broiler. But he couldn't take his eyes off the photo. None of them could.

"Is this something you guys want?" John asked the boys. He saw them nod in reply, some emphatic about it and others less demonstrative, sort of thoughtfully adding their assent.

"Then you're going to have to work to get there," the coach said. "It's different now. You're the team to beat. Everybody knows about Toms River."

A brief silence engulfed the All-Stars as they took in John's words. The coach took off his ballcap, rubbed a hand through his salt-and-pepper hair, adjusted his wire-framed glasses. He let the silence linger for a few seconds, then gestured again toward the photograph and raised his arms, palms up, toward the boys circled around him. He then bent to the ground to pick up the picture. "Think about it now," he said. "And then don't think about it again until we get there."

WITH THE IMAGE ROLLED UP and set aside, the boys of Toms River American got down to business. The district tournament was to begin in less than two weeks, and for the most part, the kids already knew what to do. Over the course of the summer of 2006, John had developed a practice routine from which he had rarely strayed since; it was a program heavy on repetition and devoid of flair. Coach John didn't want a team of acrobats. He wanted a team full of players who were firmly grounded in the basic elements of the game: the cleanly fielded ball; the direct throw; a disciplined swing of the bat; a well-located pitch.

"We don't want you to make the super plays," he told the kids bluntly. "You don't need to do that. We just want you to make the routine plays every time they happen, because they happen all the time.

"Hey, all I need from you is the six good innings. That hasn't changed from last year. Okay? So let's go."

Johnny Puleo sprinted out to shortstop, Scotty to third base. Austin Higgins ran to first base, where he would share the drills with Chris Gulla. Andrew and Vinny took turns at second. From just in front of home plate, Ryan Fabricatore, who was to catch most of the innings for the Toms River team this summer, began firing the ball around the infield, from one position to another.

"Four! Four! Four!" Ryan screamed as he threw the ball to Scotty, his instructions indicating that Scotty was to get the ball back to him (home plate being the fourth base, or "four" in baseball parlance) as quickly as he could. As soon as he received it, Ryan pulled the ball out of his catcher's mitt and threw to Johnny, who rifled it back to Ryan. Back and forth the throws went, one position at a time, round and round like the spokes of a wheel—a series of routine tosses that over time would feel like just that to the infielders: second nature, routine. In a game, they might need to make one of those throws to give Ryan a chance to tag out a runner trying to score, or to step on home for a force-out if the bases were loaded. John wanted to know—he needed to know—that his players could make those throws in their sleep. They would make hundreds of such throws between now and the first game of the district tournament.

And if you were to go looking for the line of demarcation between the regular season and the All-Star tournaments in Little League, this was as good a place to start as any. The expanded drills were the baseball equivalent of advanced math. For John and the other coaches, the regular season was always the time to dial back their strategies to the basic precepts of the sport. Even at the Majors level, most of practice was devoted to elementary lessons in throwing, fielding and hitting. John spent his days correcting kids' pitching motions; he showed them how to square their bodies to home plate as they stepped into the batter's box; he reminded them to run *through* the first-base bag rather than merely running to it. It was one thing at a time, one day at a time. The entire season was viewed as one ongoing teaching opportunity, which was fairly close to the description Little League International might choose to define its purpose to the mass of children and adolescents who filled its coffers every year with their entry fees. In that context, the big picture was always easy enough to see: The coaches were working with a wildly diverse cross-section of talent, which often included kids from many different grades on the same team, and they had to keep it simple to have any chance of succeeding on a group level. The only other alternative was a series of one-on-one coaching sessions, and there wasn't time for that. The point of the drills was a basic sort of reliable. During the regular season, reliable was good enough.

But All-Stars were different—markedly, thrillingly different. John emphasized the basics with his Toms River Americans, yes, but these were the basics of high-level competition, not of ordinary play. Those multiple spins around the throwing wheel of the infield were designed specifically to produce players like Scotty and Johnny who could snuff out a rally on the spot, not simply by fielding a ground ball and firing it to home plate, but by fielding it and firing it home *perfectly*. There was a difference. It was the difference between good and great. It was the difference between out and safe. As the boys themselves had learned the summer before, it was the difference between win and lose.

John wasn't working with tots. He sure wasn't babysitting. He was coaching 12- and 13-year-old boys who, in the way they played baseball, were mature beyond their ages. They would play for John the way men played for their college or professional coaches and managers. They would get out on the field and get right to it in practice, because that was what John had demanded of them in those long, hot days of the summer of 2006. They were still kids, no doubt, but right now they were kids with a plan.

Having taken up his place in the outfield, Quintin quickly started getting the same treatment as his infield teammates, challenged to consistently repeat his throws from center field to second base, to third base, and to home. "Run it again!" John said. "Three! Three! Three!" he shouted, meaning the throw was to go to third base. From his spot in center, Quintin drifted easily under a fly ball that John had hit in his direction; he made the catch and threw a perfect strike to Scotty at third base. The transaction elicited no response from anyone else on the field, because they were so used to good throws coming from Quintin—or "Q," as many of his teammates called him. Q could deliver that same throw as many times as anyone wanted. He was one of Toms River's great weapons, an outfielder who could be depended on to track down any fly ball and throw out a runner trying to advance a base or score a run. Quintin had already made this throw at least a thousand times. The kid knew it by heart.

After a while, Vinny left the infield drill and ran to join the outfielders in practicing their throws. Billy Sullivan was out there, and Mo Volk, and now Quintin, too. "Let's do it right," Vinny said, to himself as much as to his teammates. These boys already understood that their summer was going to be spent primarily in the outfield, because most of them had played for John the year before and had been assigned their positions then. There were only two newcomers, Clayton Kapp and Drew Fanara, and both would likely play outfield as well. This was most definitely not how it worked during Little League's regular season, when kids were routinely moved from spot to spot on the field—now first base, now left field, now catcher—in an effort to equalize opportunities for each player. Here, now, John needed the best players at the best spots, and as encouraging as he was by nature, he had no intention of placating anyone if it even briefly put the All-Stars at a competitive disadvantage.

From the infield/outfield drills, the boys went through their basic coverages, with John reminding them who had the responsibility for each type of play that might arise on defense. The catchers worked on their throws to second base in case an opponent tried to steal, with John shouting out either "Toms!" or "River!" to tell his infielders which one of them—second base or shortstop—would be taking the throw and making the tag. They practiced crashing in from first and third base to pounce on a bunt, with Scotty or Chris suddenly charging at full speed toward home to field the ball and look for a play.

The pitchers peeled off, one by one, to go to a side bull pen and get in their practice-day tosses. Jerry Volk, Mo's dad, was there; he had gone early to his job at the Environmental Protection Agency in Philadelphia so that he could get back to Toms River in time. Jerry set up a hitting station off a tee, and Paul Fabricatore set up another station on the other side of the field—a "soft toss" area where Paul would repeatedly lob baseballs underhanded to the waiting hitter, who pounded them into a safety net, one swing after another. John and Scott Ringel threw batting practice on the field, alternating when they grew arm-weary and pulling in Jerry when needed. And on and on it went, with the players rotating through each of the hitting stations, finishing up with the live practice against the coaches.

"Drive one, Q!" Vinny shouted. Quintin obliged by cracking hit after hit into the outfield, usually in the gaps between where some of the kids had been set up to shag the balls and throw them back in so that John could reload his supply. Quintin's stroke was pure and clean, the contact solid, his smile broad. It was hard to imagine, watching him lacerate Coach John's pitches with such batting-practice ease, that he would ever struggle to get a hit in a game.

John cranked up the intensity by moving in closer, to within 20 or 25 feet of home plate, so that he could pump fastballs at each player and see how the hitters reacted to the pitches getting to them so quickly. Johnny stepped in, flicking his wrists quickly at each pitch so that he could get his bat through the strike zone in time to make contact. Scotty took his cuts; he whipped his bat back into hitting position after each swing like a hunter reloading a rifle. The sweat glistened on John's face and underneath the bill of his baseball cap, but he didn't stop throwing.

Both John and his players knew that this wasn't being done for the coach's amusement: at the 12-year-old level, there were going to be guys who could throw in excess of 65 miles per hour from a pitcher's mound that was only 46 feet away from home plate, which was like a fastball in the pros coming in to a batter at more than 90 miles an hour.

Toms River had to be quick, focused and attentive to put the ball in play—and it would. It had to be smart on defense and completely capable of making that routine play routinely—and it would. John's workouts and his direction made as much very clear. There would be no excuses for not living up to this set of elite basics. This first workout was the start.

But even before the first All-Star gathering of 2007, Puleo's practices were something of a legend among the denizens of Toms River Little League. He had put the system in the summer before. His workouts were long, intense, action-driven and, over time, very familiar. They started the same way each day and continued through those same fielding, throwing and batting drills each day, and only when things had gone exceptionally well—which turned out to be fairly often—did John allow the players to finish up with an intramural hitting contest.

Time itself seemed to expand during the workouts. As Jerry Volk noted with a chuckle, "If John told the parents that practice would be done at ten thirty, no one would even start showing up until at least eleven. They all knew." Last year, with nearly a month to get ready for district competition, the 11-year-old All-Stars worked out only once a day, but that single practice routinely dragged on past the three-hour mark. This summer, with not even two weeks of preparation time before the first game, John had informed the parents that the team would be going with two-a-day workouts, morning and evening, skipping only the high heat of the afternoon.

◆ ◆ ◆

THE LAYOUT OF THE SUMMER was simple, albeit head-spinning. Toms River first had to survive its district competition, District 18, in which it might have to win seven games to outlast its brutally competitive local rivals, teams from Jackson and Holbrook and Manchester and other close-by townships. Once the boys had won that, they would move on to a section tournament, one of four such playoffs in the state. The four section winners would then proceed to the state championship; the state champion got to move on to the six-team Mid-Atlantic Regional; and that regional tournament, held in Bristol, Connecticut, would produce a winning team whose reward was one of the eight U.S. berths in the Little League World Series.

The whole thing happened gradually and then suddenly, with one tournament bleeding right into the next. From the beginning of practice in mid-June, it was barely a two-month span to get through all those levels—district, section, state, and region—and arrive in Williamsport for the opening parade on August 17. By the time the Little League World Series was over 10 days later, it would be just about time to go back to school.

For Pauly Schifilliti, one of John's important returning All-Stars, the implications of his coach's rigorous practice schedule, combined with the tournament games themselves, were obvious: Nobody involved with this team was going to be doing much this summer besides playing baseball. That's the way it had gone last year, and last year there was only the one practice per day. Now, going morning and night, the hours in between those two practices would be spent mostly recovering and staying indoors, out of the humidity. Pauly figured he could barely go to the beach unless he and his family went in a major hurry, because it would be after noon before he left, and he had to be back, ready for another workout, by perhaps 5 p.m. He might get lucky and catch a movie in the early afternoon. He could take a short swim, but Coach John had always told the guys not to spend too much time in the pool on baseball days because it left them sore-eyed and sluggish. Even though Pauly knew John was talking about game days, he thought the basic rule ought to apply all summer. There was too much at stake to be goofing off or ruining your chances.

But when Pauly considered the big picture, he didn't mind the sacrifice. "It's worth it," he said. He had no trouble believing that his team was good enough and deep enough to make a run at the Little League World Series, and so the work schedule simply became one more reality; it was the price of admission for the ride. Pauly knew how good the team was. He was there for every pitch of the summer of '06. This team had already broken through; it already knew it could win close games and outwork other teams. It seemed fated for Toms River American to be winning.

THE PHOTO ITSELF HAD BEEN a gift. When Anthony Schifilliti, Pauly's father, traveled to Williamsport on business not long after the 2006 summer was over, he spotted the poster-size overhead shot in a store and bought it on an impulse, thinking that it would be the perfect year-ending present for John from his family.

"It was just a way of saying thank-you for everything he was doing," Anthony said. "The coaches, they do so much. They put in the time. It was just to give something back, 'cause he gives so much—it's just so much time."

Anthony, a dark, handsome, middle-aged man who was in the process of getting his young family moved across town into a new place, was one of the legion of Little League parents who didn't have that kind of time. Frankly, he wondered how anyone did, which made him appreciate John all the more. When the All-Stars went those 56 straight days in the summer of '06, either practicing or playing every day and sometimes driving hours round-trip for a single game, it was impossible to conceive that the coaches could continually show up for baseball duty without either getting fired from their real jobs or losing their businesses. John ran his own printing company, and Jerry made the round-trip to Philadelphia each day. The logistics alone were overwhelming. The practices were always on, and on game days John fell into the habit of having his team work out at its own Mapletree facility, before loading the boys into cars for the trip to whatever town happened to be hosting that round of the tournament. By the time of the sectional playoffs, which were being held nearly an hour's drive away, the Americans sometimes found themselves getting ready for a Little League game four hours before it was scheduled to be played. If it was a night game, the Little League families might not roll back into their driveways until eleven or later. And win or lose, there was always practice the next day.

It was crazy. It was obviously too much. But it was working.

Around Toms River, such a rubric had been in place for a while. When the first teams starting winning at epic levels in the 1990s, the newspapers were filled with stories of high-intensity practices, and of coaches—and parents—who arranged extended leaves from their jobs to follow their kids around the state, and then the region, and then the country. Mike Gaynor, the coach of those Williamsport-bound teams, closed his 10 athletic-shoe stores for a couple of weeks, costing himself thousands of dollars in back-to-school shopping; he needed to spend his time on the Little League team, and something had to give. Another coach had a coworker cover for him for 34 straight days, all so he would never have to miss a single moment of the adventure. Parents often put their lives on hold, believing that they might never see their sons play baseball at such an exciting event again. They all understood—and agreed—that if you were going to win big, it would take some time away from other things. That was the deal.

John always joked about it, waving away the comments about his constant schedule crunch and cheerfully agreeing, "Yeah, yeah—it's nuts!" to anyone who brought up the subject or asked him, often seriously, if he was going to be okay. For nearly 20 years, John had run his printing and design company, Beta Graphics, out of an office in nearby Manasquan, and he had built it from the ground up, routinely piling up 60- and 70-hour weeks in the early years. Now, with longtime clients scattered across the United States and reorders comprising more of his business than ever, John had gained flexibility in his schedule and control over his hours. He could make the decision to leave the office and head to a Little League practice—and so he did, day after day, cutting out early in the afternoon and promising himself he would make up the work on the back side. After the extended All-Star run in '06, John's first two full days back in the office were spent with his bookkeeper, trying to figure out if his printing company was broke or he was just going crazy. After so many weeks when Puleo was either absent entirely or functioning with his mind elsewhere, the only thing John was sure of was that it was still his business, because the print jobs and the bills were still piling up.

He accepted the trade-off, though, and very happily. In this, John was not alone. No matter what town or what league you visited, there were a few constants when it came to Little League, and one of them was that baseball had its hooks not only in the kids but in a significant percentage of the parents. It dug in emotionally. Its demands weren't always reasonable. It certainly didn't always prompt reasonable responses in the adults, whose collective contribution, in theory, was to facilitate a bunch of kids playing an organized game.

But once it was agreed that they were going to keep score, it wasn't only the players who wanted to win. The emotional investment was an infection that quickly spread among the coaches, the parents, the community—and never more obviously than in Toms River, the home of a Little League World Series championship team whose players and coaches, local demigods, still hung out in these parts. Those players, by now into their college years and beyond, functioned as living reminders of what was possible and therefore expected. Williamsport was no mere notion. A Toms River team, you see, had once won it all.

That team, Toms River *East* American, completed a mind-blowing sequence of events in 1998 by shocking heavily favored Japan in the World Series title game. The triumph remained the single most galvanizing moment in the history of the township. It lent to Mike Gaynor, the owner of those shoe stores, a sheen of coaching wisdom and local achievement that the passage of a decade did not dull in the slightest.

More than that, though, the victory was part of one of the most statistically improbable runs in Little League lore. Three times in five years, a Gaynor-coached Toms River East team of 12-year-olds made it all the way to Williamsport—in 1995, 1998 and again in 1999. It was an achievement unlikely to happen even once in the history of the average baseball-playing town, no matter how good or how determined. Fate was that strong.

Three times in five years? Most towns, if they made a Little League World Series even once, would talk about it forever. You'd see it on every signpost leading into the place. The odds are so thoroughly against the accomplishment that a trip to Williamsport annually assumes the characteristics of a wonderful fluke for the happily shocked towns whose teams somehow find themselves there. Yet Toms River East got there three times, almost before anyone realized what was happening.

The town got a baseball nickname out of that run— The Beast of the East—and a gorilla-suited mascot that became a cause célèbre around the baseball-loving country. With a population of slightly more than 90,000 and a location next to the better-known Jersey Shore destination of Seaside Park, Toms River suddenly was on the map for doing something great. "Thanks to baseball, people in foreign countries have heard of Toms River," former mayor Paul Brush once said. In interviews, of which he gave many related to Little League alone, the mayor referred to the 1998 championship as "our jewel, our crowning glory," and there was no questioning the sincerity in that statement.

And the run of success wasn't over. When a team from John Puleo's side of town came within a single game of making it to Williamsport again in 2005—that is, came within a whisker of making it four World Series trips for a single town in 10 years—the reputation was set in stone: Toms River was a baseball factory, producing little winners as if off an assembly line. It was just a matter of time before a new squad of Toms River kids won again, bringing broad acclaim to the area the way the teams before had done.

The '98 team was the one they all still talked about, because it was that team that had won it all. Here in 2007, that squad was less than a year from celebrating its tenth anniversary, with reunions and newspaper articles, updates on the players, and a full rehashing of the magical summer that had changed everything in Toms River. John Puleo, and the parents and coaches and players around him, were looking to add a postscript to that tale, and they had their reasons for believing it might just happen.

Pauly certainly agreed. Based on everything he had seen last summer, he felt confident that he was playing on the best

Little League team in the area, with the best chance to run the table. It seemed impossible that any collection of 12-year-olds was as loaded as his crew. Pauly had been watching Scotty play ball for years, seen Scotty's pitching velocity ratchet up and up and up. He knew that Scotty would be throwing bullets this summer. Johnny's glove at shortstop was solid—and his pitching was much better than it had been a year ago. Pauly had faith that Quintin would come up big, because he had just spent the regular season watching Q hit balls over the fence and play the outfield with his usual excellence. And Pauly believed in himself. He had pitched a lot this spring, and although his arm was beginning to feel a little tired, he had never pitched better in his life.

Like the other guys, Pauly had put in his hours over the winter, logging his workout time beside his fellow American All-Stars. All the kids, even the ones like Pauly who played basketball or wrestled, had found time to make Coach John's strength-and-conditioning sessions from November to March over at the Hit Dogs indoor baseball academy, a nice training facility inside a nondescript building on the way out of town. John had made arrangements for a specialist to work with the players, part of his overall plan not to let the momentum and chemistry of 2006 disintegrate simply because the weather turned. He also had founded a non–Little League "travel" team, comprising the same kids, in order to guarantee more baseball action up and down the Jersey Shore in the fall. The players and their families, now loosely organized as a group called the Bengals, turned to Hit Dogs as a warm, dry facility at which to get together every Saturday through the freezing months.

The Hit Dogs academy was the kind of place that didn't even exist when Mike Gaynor's teams were first covering the town in Little League glory. But times had changed. Specialization was now a fact of life in youth sports, whether anyone liked it or not. If you weren't putting in your work in the winter, you were almost guaranteed to get your doors blown off come the following summer by some collection of baseball maniacs that had refused to relax through the down time. The same was true for the soccer teams, the football teams— every sport had crossed that line a long time ago. Winning, even winning at Little League baseball, was now a matter of grim-faced work and repetition as much as of attitude. It was one thing to have the right players in the right places; it was something altogether different to have them practicing fiercely enough, often enough, to capitalize on that. If John's team came up short, the coach decided, it wasn't going to be because the kids hadn't put in the time.

Like Pauly, Vinny didn't mind the extra work. He liked his team, liked its chances. The group had finished third in the state of New Jersey as 11-year-olds—and, really, they easily could have won a state title. They ran out of pitching at the end—ran out of most everything, at the finish, but pitching most of all—and that could be corrected. The Toms River Americans, in fact, had won their first game at the state tournament last summer, hadn't they? Scotty Ringel had pitched an incredible game, and it was a 9–0 blowout of Washington Township. The team was on such a high, even Coach John allowed himself to start thinking about his victory speech, trying to frame the words he would use to thank his coaches and parents.

Two quick defeats later, Toms River was done for the summer—"two and barbecue," as John recalled it—but the boys had only begun to imagine the possibilities. They all had this feeling that their accomplishments were but a prelude to 2007, when they could really go somewhere in Little League. The core of the team was intact. The boys had proved they could win and win big. It wasn't long after the state tournament ended in 2006 that the boys began to talk in earnest about Williamsport, to say the words out loud. Nobody minded saying them. Nobody worried about a jinx in Toms River.

The talk didn't bother the coach, either. John could have dampened the level of expectation or shouted down the bravado, but why bother? First of all, that was the fun of it—the dreaming—and John knew that it was impossible to quell the talk in his town, anyway. When it came to Little League in Toms River, he spent almost no time dwelling on the difficulties: the politics of choosing the teams; the town's habit of circling around its own history; the desperate, lurching attempts by some of the parents to place their children's names on All-Star rosters. The politics existed, sure. John knew that, because his wife, Diane, dealt with it routinely in her volunteer positions within the league, and because they both were aware of how much nonsense the ever-patient president of Toms River Little League, Joe Cudia, had to put up with on a weekly basis. But none of the machinations mattered to John. By choosing to coach, he had remained largely outside the fray—beyond the realm of the parents who complained about the team their child had been placed with, the kid who couldn't play for a certain coach, all that. Little League, the way John used it, was very nearly a pure good.

John had coached Johnny since he was five years old playing tee-ball, and had stuck with his firstborn through every level. In more recent years, he had been lucky enough to be around Johnny for four straight seasons at Little League Majors, the highest level of regular season competition, helping with and coaching the Red Sox. Johnny's June birth date had guaranteed him a roll-around year as, basically, a 13-year-old playing All-Stars on the "11–12" team as designated by Little League International. Johnny was older, but, like Scotty, he was just young enough on the calendar, and so he—and his dad—got that fourth year together. Despite the friction such a father-son coaching arrangement naturally created, Johnny didn't seem to mind John's presence; he was used to it. Now, John was entering his second summer as the All-Star coach, and he was getting his first crack at a 12-year-old, Williamsport-eligible team—with his own son as a principal player.

Beyond Johnny there was John's son Matt, just 10 years old and already a Red Sox player as well, and his daughter Sophia, who had turned 7 and was clearly an athlete in her own right. Even Diane was heavily involved in the league, serving as a liaison for coaches in some of the younger age groups. Diane had long ago come to understand that baseball was a focal point in the Puleo family dynamic, and rather than stand off to the side, she had chosen to jump in. She could handle herself in situations in which some plain talk was called for, and she knew how to calm down a coach and soothe the feelings of a wounded parent.

And his family's involvement pleased John tremendously. Diane's willingness to let him spend unrecoverable hours at the Mapletree complex gave him a green light for his passion. He was sure that he was where he wanted to be. He had years and years of coaching left, and he was starting to get pretty good at it, and he wasn't about to let go. He fairly loved the experience at every turn. Maybe it was he who had the grip on baseball, not the other way around.

JOHN BROUGHT OUT THE PHOTOGRAPH again, and he stood back for a minute or two while the boys of Toms River American, under a late afternoon sky near the end of their first official practice together as the 12-year-old All-Stars, got a good, long look at Williamsport. Over at one of the fence lines, Scott Ringel thought to himself, "Not bad." He liked the motivating tactic. Scott had been around this group of kids, or at least the core of it, since the boys were 9 years old, playing together in their first tournament in nearby Barnegat, when they barely had a clue what they were doing. He credited John with teaching the team how to win, how to prepare for winning and expect it. Before John took over, the team had done well as 9- and 10-year-olds without ever actually getting all the way to a title. At every stop, the boys from Jackson had come between the Americans and their goals. It was Coach Puleo who finally had gotten the boys over the hump last year, including a victory over Jackson in the district finals that people were still talking about. Everything about John's practices and pregame routines pointed toward a winning approach; his energy and enthusiasm rubbed off on everyone. You'd have a hard time being around the coach and not concluding that it was, in fact, a fantastic day for baseball. Now that you thought about it, there was no reason to expect anything other than massive success from this team. Above everything else, Scott believed, that kind of broad optimism was the magic of Coach John.

But Scott was first and foremost a realist. He knew that Chris Gulla was ailing, as a result of two separate injuries Chris had dealt with this spring. He knew that Pauly had been overused as a pitcher during the regular season, to the point that Pauly didn't have a lot left in his valuable right arm. Scott certainly understood growth rates and the unpredictability of the preadolescent body; his son Scotty seemed to be the only one on the squad who was appreciably bigger since last year. He understood what a fine line separated winning from losing at the youth level, and the many different ways things could go wrong—or right—in the blink of the eye.

When the boys were 11, just about everything went their way, and it happens like that sometimes. You get on a roll, and the breaks start falling in your favor—or maybe you make your own breaks with inspired play, with full effort. Either way, getting to the state tournament had felt more like an adventure than a grind. It was so special—and, Scott believed, the kind of feeling that the team could have only once. After that, winning was going to be work. Scott loved baseball, but he was no nostalgic. Last summer, glorious as it was, was over.

Scott already had seen some of the teams around the district this year that Toms River would have to get past—the ones, for that matter, that already had marked the Americans as the team they needed to take down. According to some of the parents, a few of those teams' coaches had scouted the Toms River Little League games during the regular season, surveying the kids, seeing how they'd changed, looking for a strategic edge to take into All-Star play.

And Scott listened to the kids themselves, listened to the guys talk about getting to the World Series. Sometimes one word, *Williamsport*, would drift out of their conversations and over to the assistant coach as he stacked the buckets of baseballs to get ready for batting practice. Scott would smile to himself and say little. He didn't want to discourage the conversation, because that's the fun of it, being able to talk and dream; but there was something unnerving about hearing the kids actually speak the word. One of baseball's unwritten rules had to do with the things players did not say out loud—for example, everyone on a team knew not to speak to a pitcher who was working on a no-hitter—and this situation, to Scott, fell squarely into that category.

Baseball's a superstitious sport, even down at the kids' level. But given the history of his town, the Williamsport talk was inevitable. It was hard to be in Toms River for even a day without understanding what the Little League teams meant to the place. You found the old articles about them framed behind glass and hung on restaurant walls. You saw the banners every time you stepped into either Little League complex, hung high from the buildings that housed the indoor practice facilities and tacked to the announcers' booths outside the playing fields—banners that explained the past successes of the respective leagues. The successes had become, on some levels, the identity of the town itself. The old squads were by now legend. Wanting to join them was almost second nature to anyone who loved the game.

Scott smiled as he watched John roll out the photograph of the World Series and let the kids' dreams begin to run unfettered. He understood why John did it. Scott only wondered if, in the end, wanting Williamsport so badly might be the exact thing that prevented the boys—and their coaches—from getting there.

CHAPTER 2

FACTORY TOWN

A FEW YEARS AGO, CHRIS CERULLO, a member of the first Toms River team ever to crash Williamsport in 1995, had his Little League World Series moment, the one that reminded him how far-reaching the legend of the town had become. In the middle of a road trip with his college baseball team, Cerullo found himself ambling through the French Quarter in New Orleans one spring evening. The team was in town to play Tulane University. Cerullo had left his hotel room wearing the T-shirt he'd grabbed out of his bag earlier in the day, an old short-sleeve with the words "Mike Gaynor's All-Star Camp" emblazoned across the front, a giveaway from Gaynor as thanks for Chris having coached at one of Gaynor's summer baseball camps a year earlier.

"I wasn't even thinking about what I was wearing—I was just running out to Mardi Gras for a while," Cerullo said. "But after a few minutes, I started noticing that I was getting looks. By the time I got around the Quarter, four or five people had come up to me and asked, 'Mike Gaynor? The Little League Mike Gaynor?'"

Cerullo paused. "That was *nine years* after we went to Williamsport."

A similar shock of recognition hit Donna Gulla near the beginning of the 2007 Little League season. In an effort to buy a bat that her son Chris wanted to use, Donna wound up on the phone with a catalog-company representative from the Midwest. When it came time to complete the order, Donna gave the woman her mailing address. "Oh, Toms River!" the representative replied. "You've got some pretty good baseball going there."

"A couple of years ago," said Hit Dogs facility owner Jack Daubert, "one of my sons was playing in a summer amateur tournament up near Boston. So we go to sit in the stands, and my wife starts talking to the mom next to her, and the mom has a kid sitting with her. So my wife gives the kid a baseball card of our son Jake.

"The kid looks at the card, turns to his dad and says, 'Jake's from Toms River. That's the greatest baseball program in the world.' They knew all about it, and about all those guys, the World Series guys. And that's how it happens. When you're talking youth baseball, it's Toms River."

Over the past decade, and with the burnishing of the legend, Toms River became the default expression of young baseball dreams in America, and its arrival to such a role was the product both of serendipitous timing and good fortune. The timing lay in the marriage of Little League baseball's inherently attractive World Series and ESPN's need for programming, two forces that joined together right around the time Cerullo and his '95 teammates were storming the castle. That, and the arrival on the scene of Mike Gaynor and his teams.

For years, nobody around Toms River knew quite what to do with Gaynor. At times, the success of the teams he had coached appeared to eclipse almost every squad that came after his, and at times, it almost seemed that Gaynor himself had become famous on the achievements of the children. It was the kids, after all, who did all the playing in Williamsport.

But Mike Gaynor's name was at the center of the most joyfully important social and cultural event ever to hit Toms River, and there was no getting around it—nor should there be. Gaynor was the right coach at the right time, with the right groups of kids, graced by the right combination of stars and role players, and alone able to use that combination to win championships, not just games. It was impossible to separate out any of the elements of the success and still arrive at three Little League World Series appearances in five years, such an odds-defying accomplishment that the results spoke for themselves. And it was those three trips to Williamsport that gave Toms River the national profile it was still carrying around in 2007, when John Puleo's team began to bear down on the legacy.

By now, you couldn't begin to understand the Toms River community without knowing about its Little League history. It no longer mattered, for example, that baseball had been the leading sport in the township long before Gaynor's teams rose to glory, nor that the three high school coaches—Kenny Frank, his brother, Bill, and Ted Schelmay—had been doing the heavy lifting for years, establishing the criteria for excellence that trickled down to the youth programs. High school success was wonderful and special, and there was no question that it drove much of the mania for the sport in town, yet it was Little League that became Toms River's calling card. Little League was what people all across the country wanted to talk about, constantly. And that all went straight back to Mike Gaynor.

"All the time, I have guys tell me that I screwed things up forever," Gaynor said. "The pressure on these coaches, what they want to do and need to do, the pressure they put on the kids, these all-weather facilities—it's all for just one objective. Everyone has that one objective, man. It's all about Williamsport."

Yet Gaynor himself never had that objective, at least not in the beginning. There was no blueprint for what happened in 1995, again in 1998 and once more in 1999. No town near Toms River had ever flirted seriously with making it to the Little League World Series.

Before the arrival of the Little League dynasty, Toms River had enjoyed a long and mostly anonymous existence at the eastern edge of Ocean County, just a bridge-crossing away from the Jersey Shore and such tourist and summer vacation spots as Seaside Park and Ortley Beach. The main road running east to the shore, State Route 37, was inundated on both sides by fast-food joints, pizza restaurants, hotels and gas stations—a full-service economy bathed in neon and screaming from elevated signs. The neighborhoods were built at a deliberate remove from the main road, and because of it the town took on the feeling of one large collection of suburbs without any real urban area connecting them. Crime was low. The schools were good. Not a lot happened.

Prior to its appearance at the Little League World Series, Toms River had made the national news twice that anyone could remember. The first time came in the 1980s, when a local businessman named Robert Marshall was charged with putting out a contract killing on his wife, a case that eventually formed the basis of writer Joe McGinniss's book *Blind Faith*. The second came in the '90s, when health officials drew a connection between advanced rates of childhood cancers in the area and a contaminated groundwater leakage around a chemical plant, a story that reverberated and roiled for years and through several lawsuits. Even in the summer of 2007, more than one person in Toms River answered a question about the town's baseball prowess by observing, "They say it's something in the water."

Baseball had no antidote for that. But Mike Gaynor's initial World Series breakthrough did represent the first bit of undiluted good news for which Toms River had ever been recognized outside of Ocean County. What Gaynor didn't realize, because no one could have known at the time, was that the town was on the front edge of a kind of cult fame that would prove surprisingly durable, and that would inform the efforts of years' worth of succeeding Toms River Little League teams.

IN 1995, GAYNOR WAS BUT another dad coaching some kids, including his son Colin, to play ball. When the All-Star season rolled around that June, he took the Toms River

East Americans in the 12-year-old division, because that was Colin's age group. The selection process for All-Stars was not terribly refined. Toms River East Little League—TRELL, for short—had split into two divisions three years earlier, and league officials devised an alphabetical strategy for dividing the players. If your last name began with the letters A through J, you were in the American League; K through Z went to the National League. Thus, Gaynor's selections were limited to those kids whose last names fell on his side of the alphabet. (Gaynor still laughs about Jimmy Principe, a wonderful player who eventually was drafted by the Arizona Diamondbacks in professional baseball—but couldn't play on Gaynor's Little League World Series team because of his last name.) Gaynor had known that he had two very good players—Colin and a boy named Jeff Frazier—and a host of kids who could play their roles and hit the ball.

Gaynor had had a hand in Little League coaching for years, and he had developed a strong sense of how he wanted his team to practice and prepare for the games. It was his own routine, born of his experience, and it emphasized the boys moving quickly from one practice station to the next: a hitting drill; a fielding drill; a throwing drill, and so on. Gaynor's All-Star team spent hours and hours on the fundamentals of hitting and pitching, because Gaynor already had decided that if his guys could score a lot, they had a chance to win some games in the difficult District 18 playoffs, and if they could pitch well, they would always have protection against those days when the bats fell silent.

He even had a coach he wanted to work with, Ken Kondeck, whose own children had long since outgrown Little

League. Kondeck still loved to coach, and he appreciated and supported the Little League model for competition. Gaynor saw Kondeck all the time around the Toms River East Little League complex during the regular season, doing routine chores, keeping scorebooks, often stopping to offer Gaynor a suggestion. When Gaynor asked him to work with the All-Star team, Kondeck agreed but insisted on remaining outside the dugout during games; he wanted to sit in the stands with the kids' parents, keeping a scorebook and making notes, allowing Gaynor to run the team on the field. The two hit it off immediately, and the kids took to Kondeck, who had so many stories to tell about the years when his kids played Little League that he quickly acquired the nickname "Gramps."

Gaynor and Kondek worked well together, and Gaynor in particular had an easy way with the kids. He was not a screamer. He found it pointless to chew out a young player over a physical mistake the boy clearly didn't mean to make. For that matter, Gaynor had decided that mistakes in general weren't worth discussing in their immediate aftermath. Emotions were too raw in the moments following a tough game; there was always a practice the next day, or the day after that, to work out such kinks. Mike was constantly focused on what came next, not on what had just happened.

"Mike is the best coach I ever had, and I had great high school and college coaches," said Chris Cerullo. "But Mike was the perfect combination for coaching kids. He never put pressure on us. He didn't yell. He let us know he supported us, and taught us the kind of stuff that helped us do our jobs better. It was really just a great time."

Still, in the summer of '95, no one was predicting any

sort of outsized success. The year before, the East Americans had won their district, but then lost two straight contests and got bounced from the section tournament. Toms River was good at baseball, and the town had a pure passion for the sport, but there was nothing in the Little League record to suggest that anything historic was about to come of it.

And then the Fence Game changed everything.

Heading into District 18 competition in the summer of '95, Gaynor felt that he had a good enough team to win some games. His son Colin was a fine all-around player, a boy with such natural athletic ability that he would one day accept a full scholarship to play football at Northeastern University. Jeff Frazier was one of three baseball-playing brothers from a family that would in time become, along with the Gaynors, the sports royalty of Toms River. But when Gaynor's East Americans quickly lost a game in the District 18 playoffs, it meant they would have to beat the same team twice in the finals to win the district and move on. Their opponent: Toms River Little League—on its own field.

The rivalry was born of simple geography and was given weight and substance because of years and years of competition. Hooper Avenue, which essentially runs from the old downtown waterfront village of Toms River north to Brick Township and beyond, neatly bisected Toms River into its two kid-baseball demographics. Parents whose homes lay west of Hooper registered their children with Toms River Little League—TRLL, for short—the one on Mapletree Road, the first youth baseball league created in the town. Anyone living on the other side of Hooper played ball with Toms River East Little League, off Windsor Avenue—the one with the newer facilities and more fields.

You wouldn't say the two leagues detested each other at that point in the town's history. In general, Toms River residents wanted to see their teams beat Jackson and Brick Township, whose baseball programs also excelled all the way up to the high school teams. But the competitive friction was already present within Toms River; and with a district championship on the line in 1995, supporters of the two Little Leagues filled the bleachers and crowded around the new outfield fence at Mapletree, lending an electric feel to a game being played mostly by sixth-graders. One of those teams was going to walk away with a title.

The new fence itself was an afterthought. When Gaynor's team won the first game to force a winner-takes-the-district finale, the showdown was the talk of the town. But a key adjustment to the outfield had indeed been made, albeit weeks earlier: TRLL had raised the height of the fence from four to six feet, partly to limit the number of fly balls that sneaked over the shorter fence and partly in response to suggestions from district administrators about how to run a better All-Star tournament. Everyone agreed that the decision was a good one: more balls stayed in the park, meaning more balls were in play. The kids saw more live action, and spent less time simply watching someone circle the bases after a medium-deep fly ball dropped beyond the fence. And the 12-year-olds seldom got cheated, anyway—their home runs were usually far beyond the park's 200-foot dimensions. There was no discernible downside. The fence wasn't even a conversation piece. Not yet.

In the championship game at the end of June, Gaynor's team grabbed an early lead, slicing base hit after base hit into the gaps between the Toms River Little League outfielders— and the coach had big and strong Jeff Frazier on the mound. Jeff was one of those kids who, on the field, looked beyond his years; he threw like the big-leaguers, with a refined pitching motion and a crisp, hard delivery, even if he threw at the speed of a child. His Toms River East teammates gave Jeff a 7–3 lead going into the bottom of the sixth and final inning, and the way he was throwing, the game looked over. TRELL was going to do the unthinkable: beat TRLL twice in a row, then hold the district championship banner aloft for a team photo right there on the enemy's home field.

In the dugout, though, Gaynor knew better than to assume anything about a Little League game. He wanted three more outs from Frazier, but he also knew that even Jeff couldn't pitch forever. It was hot and humid, and when you started talking about 12-year-old boys, things could change in a hurry—and, as if on cue, they did. After looking so good for so many innings, Jeff suddenly started to run out of steam. The TRLL batters found the holes in the field on three straight hits, and then another single. Just like that, the score was 7–5, the TRLL parents were on their feet and the home team's dugout was alive and buzzing. TRLL had two runners on base and a great young batter, Mike McTamney, coming to the plate. McTamney was one of a legion of Toms River players who would ultimately succeed on both the collegiate and professional levels, going from school to semipro ball to a contract with the Philadelphia Phillies. And in this moment, McTamney was up to being a hero. He swung at one of Jeff's fastballs, his bat making perfectly solid contact, and he struck a monster shot to dead center field.

Coaching from the dugout, Gaynor felt his stomach fall as he immediately recognized it for what it was: a three-run homer to end the game and win the district for TRLL. But Gaynor, too, had forgotten about the fence. McTamney's ball, a line drive that rose briefly and then began to descend, easily would have cleared the old, four-foot barrier. Instead, it smacked the new fence at the very top, and came ricocheting right back at stunned center fielder Chris Cerullo, who quickly fielded it on a bounce and rifled the ball back to the infield, where a relay throw to home plate prevented the runner at third from trying to score. Instead of an electrifying, title-capturing blow, the hit had scored only one run, meaning Gaynor's team still had a 7–6 lead.

But the strange sequence of the play was not over. McTamney noticed the throw home and bolted for second base. The Toms River East catcher threw the ball to Danny Gallagher at second to try to get McTamney—but as soon as the throw left his hand, the runner from third headed home, trying to score the tying run. Danny, focused on receiving the throw at second, heard the commotion from the crowd, and abruptly looked up to see the runner sprinting home. Danny fired a perfect strike from second base to the plate. The runner was out by two steps. Gaynor and the Toms River East kids had won the district championship—just like that. In jubilation and disbelief, the boys fell into a pile around the pitcher's mound, leaping on top of one another, trying to take in what had just happened.

"The ball hits the top of the fence," Gaynor said, still

remembering the sequence almost second by second, frame by frame, more than a decade after it occurred. "McTamney's ball is out of the park before they raise the fence, you understand? It's way out. Game over. We don't get out of the district. And no offense to the Toms River kids—they were a good team, and I loved every one of their players, who I got to know down the line as time went on—but they wouldn't have gone as far as we did if they had won. Still, they were going to win it, no doubt—"

Gaynor paused, relishing the memory, and then broke into a smile that lit up his eyes.

"The ball hits the fence," he repeated. "They're still cryin'."

THE DISTRICT CHAMPIONSHIP GAME GOT Toms River East rolling, and when the boys blew through the section playoffs to advance to the state tournament, it meant a 60-mile drive each way to Gloucester City, which was certainly the farthest the players and parents had ever traveled for a Little League game. Still, neither Gaynor nor his players had any strong sense of what was to come. They knew they were playing good baseball, and both Colin and Jeff had been pitching beautifully; but everything felt like such a close call. All the games could go either way—like the first game at Sectionals, when it took yet another relay throw from the outfield to peg a runner from Wall Township at home plate and preserve a close victory for TRELL. And for all that, there still was no real buzz in Toms River, because there was no history to suggest anything great was about to happen.

"But it was a fun time," Gaynor said. "We had to go to Gloucester City every day. It was the middle of a heat wave. We met every day at three o'clock down at the Little League to do batting practice and everything, and we'd get back home from the games at midnight every night, and I'd go jump in the pool to cool down."

The Toms River boys lost their first game to North Hunterdon, a team that featured two brothers of future Major League player Jack Cust. But then Gaynor's pitching plan began to click. With Jeff and Colin alternating assignments on the mound, Toms River reeled off four straight victories to take the state title, including a 3–2 decision over a team from Audubon whose players would go on years later to form the number-one-ranked high school team in the state. And Gaynor's team finished in style, pitching Jeff and then Colin in whipping the Hunterdon team twice in a row for the title—just as it had done to Toms River Little League in the district tournament.

THE BOYS FROM EAST WENT on to the regional tournament in Bristol, Connecticut, and Toms River parents and fans were slowly warming to the idea that they really had something going with their Little League team. The regional tourney thoroughly reinforced that optimism. Simply put, Gaynor's team rolled. Jeff Frazier felt as if he couldn't do any wrong—his pitches were true and his batting stroke just right—and he and Colin formed an unbeatable combination on the mound. The result was a surreal, outlandish sort of success—nothing but wins, five straight, and by a combined score of 43–5. Gaynor and his players spent the entire period in a sort of daze, constantly looking for the team that would knock them off, but that team never arrived. Toms River fans filled four buses for the trip to Bristol for the regional final, and it was a three-hour ride for what turned out to be a one-hour game. The championship went to Toms River East by an 11–0 score over a team from Delaware, and, in an ongoing astonishment, Gaynor's players rushed the field to celebrate the inconceivable. They were headed for Williamsport.

But although the kids still had surprise on their side, the adults around them were already advancing the line of expectation. On the eve of that finale in Bristol, a Little League official called the Toms River parents together in an effort to prepare them for what was to come. "Folks, I think at this time next week you're going to be on national TV," the official said. "This is the best team I've ever seen up here." The implication was clear: Gaynor's boys were on a direct path to the title game of the Little League World Series. In the room, some of the mothers burst into tears, overcome by the thought. Gaynor fidgeted in his seat, trying to figure whether the team was worthy of such a projection. But Jeff and Colin and their teammates looked strong enough for the man's prediction to come true.

What happened instead was almost an object lesson in how fragile the whole World Series dream truly was. After splitting its first two games in Williamsport, Gaynor's boys ran into a club from Spring, Texas, that Gaynor still believes is the best Little League team he ever coached against, and Toms River dropped an 11–10 decision that ultimately prevented the boys from reaching the U.S. championship game. They also lost the contest in gut-wrenching fashion, for which Gaynor felt responsible.

In the top of the sixth and final inning, with his team down 9–6, Chris Cerullo had come to the plate. The bases were loaded. Cerullo swung at the first good fastball he saw, and the ball shot off his bat as if fired from a gun. It easily cleared the outfield wall, and Cerullo circled the bases with a grand slam that stunned the Texans into silence and gave Toms River East a 10–9 lead. Suddenly, all Gaynor's boys needed were three outs to win and advance to the U.S. final.

The problem was, it wasn't Jeff Frazier's day. Jeff had been struggling on the mound against Texas's oversized and aggressive hitters; in fact, he had allowed all nine runs. But Gaynor, after thinking it over, sent Frazier out to pitch the bottom of the sixth. Mike believed that Jeff would somehow muscle up and get the three outs he needed. The boy was such a fierce competitor that Gaynor couldn't imagine him giving back the lead that Cerullo had just gotten for his team. But Frazier was simply done. Jeff quickly gave up a couple of hits and the tying run. By the time Gaynor finally went out and replaced him, Texas was back in the game. Colin Gaynor was on the mound for only a few minutes before one of his pitches got past the catcher and rolled to the backstop, allowing a Texas player to race home from third base with the winning run. The Toms River dream, which had really only been stoked to a full fire the week before, abruptly died. The boys were finished.

It was a hero's welcome all the same when they came

home. The boys returned to New Jersey with the good wishes of a town for their exuberance and persistence, and proclamations from city officials—a real celebration. They had made the Little League World Series, after all, and that alone was almost impossible to fathom. Jeff and Colin and Chris were treated by family and friends as if their ability to play baseball conferred upon them a sort of special magic. They became different from other players, even, because of the unique nature of their experience, and the success they had enjoyed would fuel their passion for baseball for years after.

But for Gaynor, the nagging feeling was that, despite the depth of his team's accomplishment, he had somehow pulled up lame at the end. The Texas game haunted him, not because his boys lost but because he wondered if his own decision to leave Jeff in the game had cost them a shot at winning the whole World Series. It was unknowable, of course, and Jeff was clearly one of Gaynor's horses on the team; in almost every instance, staying with Jeff would be the right thing to do. But Gaynor carried his doubts with him back to Toms River. Even amid the celebrations and congratulations, he wondered about the choice he had made, wondered what it would have felt like to win just one more game, or perhaps one more after that.

Gaynor thought about the World Series with a bittersweet longing, thinking about the game that got away. He didn't know he would get another chance to make all the right moves, and just three years later.

◆ ◆ ◆

WHAT WAS DIFFERENT ABOUT THE miracle of 1998 was that, right from the beginning, Mike Gaynor knew what he had. Coming out of the Little League regular season, he already saw that his All-Star roster was going to be loaded. He had some established stars, Todd Frazier, Jeff's wildly talented younger brother, and a boy named Scott Fisher, a left-handed pitcher and batter who was easily one of the best players at his age Gaynor had ever seen. Gaynor's younger son Casey, Colin's brother, was 11 years old but clearly good enough to play on the older All-Star team. Mike saw that he had great role players like Brad Frank and Eric Campesi, Chris Cardone and Mike Belostock. The 1998 Toms River East Americans were full of talent and energy.

And Gaynor not only knew where he wanted it to go; he felt that he knew how to get there. He had come to conclude that, as he put it, "The hardest part is not necessarily that the kids don't know what to expect, but that the coaches don't know what to expect. The hardest part is having two weeks to get ready and assemble twelve kids, decide what needs to get done and who's going to play where. All-Star teams lose because of coaching."

Gaynor, by contrast, knew his roster and knew the All-Star drill. He had spent much of the spring season preparing for this, figuring who he wanted at which position. He had three excellent pitchers in Todd, Scott and Casey. He knew how to make those two weeks of practice work. And when Toms River East sliced through both the district and section tournaments, Gaynor realized he was right about the quality of the roster he put together. What a few years before seemed so implausible now was taken on faith: Toms River East was certainly good enough to be in the New Jersey State tournament—and for that matter ought to be able to win it.

In the end, though, Gaynor's team needed another classic break to get to Williamsport. The break came in the state tournament against an opponent from Cherry Hill, the strongest team the Toms River boys had seen all summer. Cherry Hill was led by a pitcher named Mike Caruso, and Casey and Scott and Todd and the rest of the Toms River players were just baffled by him. Caruso threw hard, and he threw a real changeup and a real curve. By the sixth inning, Cherry Hill had a 2–1 lead, and Caruso looked all but invincible.

The one chink in his armor, actually, was that Caruso threw so hard his own catcher was having problems hanging on to the ball. Several times during the game, Caruso uncorked pitches that sailed past or bounced under the catcher's mitt. Up until the sixth inning, Cherry Hill was saved in every one of those situations by the fact that the backstop had been built very close to the batter's box, meaning the overthrows and underthrows simply caromed off the stop and back toward the field of play.

But with Caruso nursing his lead in the sixth inning, fate intervened. On a hit by Casey, teammate Gabe Gardner tried to score from second base, but the throw home beat him handily. Gabe got caught in a rundown and was eventually tagged out—but during the rundown Casey had alertly scooted all the way around to third base. Even though Gabe was out, Toms River East still had a runner in scoring position. It wasn't much, considering Caruso was on the mound, but at least it was something.

It turned out to be something huge. Caruso was throwing so hard that Mike Gaynor doubted his hitters were even seeing the ball; they had struck out 13 times already when R. J. Johansen came up to bat for Toms River East, with two outs and the score still 2–1. But Caruso suddenly fired a fastball over the catcher's head, and this time it was the Toms River boys who caught the lucky break. Rather than hitting the backstop, Caruso's pitch struck one of the metal poles that held the structure together, and the ball ricocheted up the first-base line, well away from home plate—the wildest of wild pitches. Chris Cardone, who had come in to pinch-run for Casey, was able to jog home and score the tying run, completely turning the momentum of the game. One inning later, Toms River East scored twice for a 4–2 victory. Cherry Hill West had been one out away from victory when it all blew up.

"Second game at State that year," Gaynor said, "and if we lose that game and go to the loser's bracket, we aren't coming back out. The field was too strong that year. That kid, Caruso, he struck out fourteen of us, because on the very next pitch it was strike three to Johansen. But the ball hit a pole. It hit a *pole*."

These are the kinds of stories that Gaynor has been telling for more than a decade, partly because they are so much fun to tell and partly because they beautifully illustrate the point that, often, the difference between fame and anonymity in the Little League tournament system is one break here or there. Gaynor wouldn't waste a moment's time feeling bad about it; he felt that his '98 team was as deserving as any in the world, and the kids were prepared to play. There was no reason for them not to go on and win. But anytime he heard teams start speaking about destiny or what they thought they were entitled to, Gaynor shook his head and chuckled. As much as he loved his roster in 1998, he never once mentioned to the players the idea of going to Williamsport. There were just so many things that could go wrong along the way. He'd been there in 1995. He had seen good teams fall, including his own. One play, maybe. One inning. Looking back, it didn't seem like so much to hang an entire town's mood upon.

But, all the same, the town was out in force to root for the Beast of the East, as Gaynor's '98 team became known. One of Gaynor's friends, Rich Cunningham, inspired by Casey's having won a gorilla as a prize at a water park one day between games in Bristol, had gone and purchased a complete gorilla outfit, which he proceeded to wear to the rest of the games that summer in Williamsport. Scores of Toms River fans were with the team right from the districts, just as soon as it became evident that Scott Fisher and Todd Frazier were performing at elite, game-changing levels of play. The boys were good, and they had Mike Gaynor on their side.

And Gaynor's own mood became considerably more buoyant when he realized that Casey not only was going to hold his own, but was going to thrive. Though still in fourth grade, Casey seemed to be improving with each game. And he could pitch. Suddenly Gaynor was a coach with options. He willingly lost a game that would have won the district title because he didn't feel he could beat the pitcher from Toms River Little League that night. Instead, Gaynor allowed his team to take the defeat in order to hold back Scott Fisher to pitch the next night, and Scott came out and pitched the 5–2 game that won the districts.

Still, no one remembered any of those details for long. They did not remember the section tournament, in which TRELL had to battle out of the loser's bracket and took a 4–3 victory in the final. They did not remember the state tourney, when Gaynor's team went down to the final, winner-take-all game against Randolph and just escaped, 7–4. People only vaguely remember that Casey Gaynor threw a three-hit shutout in the East Region semifinal in Bristol, and that Scott Fisher tossed a no-hitter to send the kids to Williamsport—a no-hitter in the regional final, a giant achievement. None of those accomplishments was as important as what happened once the Beast of the East finally did get to the Little League World Series. And the plain truth is that, without a victory over Japan in the international championship, people might only barely be remembering it still.

Mike Gaynor's team in 1998 was a perfect mix of talent, enthusiasm, coaching and—so critical—the right stars in the right places. With Todd, Scott and Casey, Gaynor had plenty of pitching. When he had to use both Casey and Scott to win the team's first game in Williamsport, a televised Sunday night battle against Michigan that dragged on for 11 innings, he simply came back with Todd the next day. Todd had more than enough left in his tank against a team from Cypress, California, and he got all the help he needed when Gabe smacked a three-run homer in the fifth inning. Toms River took a 4–2 victory to give it two wins in two tries, and the next day Casey came back with a complete-game victory over North Carolina. Todd blasted a home run. Toms River was 3–0 and in the U.S. championship game, and the boys were almost making it look easy.

Someone different turned in a great performance almost every day that summer—maybe a pitcher, or maybe someone like Mike Belostock, who didn't hit a home run during the regular season but suddenly started rifling balls over fences as an All-Star. It might be someone like Gabe, with his huge home run to beat Cypress, or even the crowd, now overrun with East supporters at Williamsport, which had practically become a Toms River camping area by the end of the week. The boys felt like they were playing a home game every day.

When it came time to face North Carolina again for the U.S. championship, the momentum was flowing completely their way. Scott Fisher was masterful on the mound, striking out ten batters in six innings. Gabe Gardner hit another home run. Todd Frazier hit a homer in the sixth inning that sealed the game. And when Scott retired the final batter on a fly ball for a 5–2 victory, the Beast of the East had officially done its 1995 predecessor one better. The first Toms River team ever to see Williamsport had won one game; the second team, the boys of 1998, had a chance to win it all.

The Little League World Series championship, against Kashima, Japan, cemented Gaynor's '98 team in Toms River lore—not only for what happened, but for how it happened. Kashima was one in a long line of powerful Japanese entries in the World Series, and the team was led by a bona fide superstar named Tetsuya Furukawa, a home-run-hitting machine. In fact, in this title game alone, Furukawa was to hit three home runs. He was simply unstoppable.

But Furukawa wasn't enough. Toms River had more than superstardom going for it. In the biggest game of their lives, Gaynor's big guns—Todd, Casey and Scott—were all wonderful, but they alone didn't win the game. Instead, a reserve named Chris Cardone took his place among the Toms River immortals. Coming off the bench and into the lineup, Cardone slugged two home runs, and the second might have been the most important hit the East Americans received all summer. The blast came in the top of the sixth inning, just after Japan had scored four times off Casey and Scott to pull to an 8–8 tie. Cardone's homer made the score 10–8, and after Todd and Scott reached base, Gabe Gardner brought them both home for a 12–8 lead. Cardone's heroics were perfect: he was the kind of player who might have been a star for another team, but he'd been lost among Toms River's lineup of home-run hitters and shutout pitchers. But on the big stage, it was Chris who took over, almost leaping his way around the bases after his homers. In the dugout, Mike Gaynor smiled to himself—a guy who had struggled to get off the bench had just delivered the biggest blow of the tournament.

When Scott finished out the sixth inning on the mound, giving up one run but finally holding the Japanese offense in check, Toms River East American Little League had a 12–9 victory, and the World Series championship. A bunch of boys' lives had just changed forever.

Thanks to Gaynor's team and the wonders of worldwide television, Toms River's reputation was being transformed by a group of kids playing a kids' game. Whereas the ABC network had been televising the World Series championship game since 1963, ESPN's involvement (and subsequent merger with ABC on sports telecasts) ramped up the coverage level year by year, with a real push beginning in the early 1990s. Such blanket coverage of early-round games and semifinals brought to the participating teams a kind of fame that no Little Leaguers had ever known, and Toms River was a recipient of that fame.

It suddenly became fashionable to mention that Toms River East had just been in Williamsport a couple of years before, in 1995—the implication being that, every couple of years, Toms River was going to be stopping by to make an appearance at the Little League World Series. The national press joined the story, following the New Jersey boys home for the parade that produced thousands of people lining the streets in Toms River, many of the fans having waited all morning for the bus that finally pulled into town a little before two in the afternoon. There were the guest shots on the talk shows, the headlines in the *New York Times*, the trip to Yankee Stadium, the appearance in the Macy's Thanksgiving Day Parade. Beat the team from Japan, and that kind of stuff will happen.

Beyond all this, though, was the profound effect on the community itself. The victory over Japan seemed to change things forever; it brought the baseball identity of the area to the front of the community's collective consciousness. As Charlie Frazier explained it, "Baseball had always been here, but with the attention and everything, the success we had with Little League turned it into a kind of fame. But the thing is, we've always been competitive here. The kids have always put a lot of pressure on themselves here, because you needed to do it just to make the high school team. You can see it from the parents and the kids. It's a baseball town."

It was a baseball town, and now the whole world knew that it was a baseball-first kind of a place. Casey Gaynor had just become the youngest player ever to start in a championship game. A kid named Joey Francheschini, at four-foot-eleven and barely 90 pounds, was one of the smallest. Chris Cardone went from unknown reserve to a kid hero so popular that he received marriage proposals from thrilled young girls. Toms River had done it—had lived out its own baseball dream. The East boys had navigated every pothole, escaped their close games. They would be remembered forever. No one even considered the possibility of an encore.

WHAT HAPPENED IN 1999, THEN, was almost too much to process. With Casey Gaynor and Eric Campesi returning, Mike Gaynor went out with another All-Star team—and ran the road to Williamsport again.

Of the three teams Gaynor coached, the '99 team was the least obviously talented. His third and fourth hitters in the lineup were playing on their first All-Star team ever. Casey and Campesi were two very good pitchers, but Gaynor couldn't find anyone else he was sure could throw in a truly critical game. He just didn't see much potential in his group.

"Of my five top guys that year," Gaynor said, "only one of them went on to play baseball all the way through high school, and that was Casey. I only had four guys who even saw the varsity field in high school. We were awful. But their disposition, their work habits—I can't say enough about those kids. They absolutely gave me everything they had."

In total defiance of the odds, that much was again enough. Gaynor by now was completely conversant in how to prepare for the different tournaments: district, section, state and regional. He knew the drills he wanted to run. He knew the signs he wanted to use. He understood some of the ways that winning teams stepped up against quality competition, and he had gotten used to the risks that accompany the playing of teams that were virtually unknown quantities before they stepped onto the field. He felt that he could get by mostly with Eric and Casey on the pitcher's mound.

And, once again, Gaynor's particular style of coaching, combining fierce and pointed workouts with a totally supportive in-game atmosphere, produced a roster that conspicuously refused to panic. Toms River East won a do-or-die game to get out of the sections, then repeated the formula in the state finals at Cherry Hill, with Chris Fontenelli driving home the winning run in the sixth inning of the championship game. Again they headed for Bristol, and again they had a pitcher take control. This time it was Casey, who by now had developed into a dominant force on the mound. He threw 23 scoreless innings in the tournament, punctuated by a 3–0 shutout of Middleboro, Massachusetts, in the Eastern Regional final, played before a raucous crowd of Toms River fans and hangers-on. The Beast of the East had done it again, three times now in five years. Again, Williamsport awaited.

The feat was almost unfathomable; in Toms River, it was a sort of sensory overload. Even Mike Gaynor struggled to come to grips with the reality of what his teams, in their little corner of the world, had achieved. In the annals of the

Little League World Series, it was virtually unique. And yet it was what happened *next*, after all of that winning, that may have sealed Toms River's fate as a town destined always to be associated with the one sport.

Why? Because heartbreak sells. And controversial heartbreak is solid gold.

With Casey and Eric leading the way, the Toms River East Americans of 1999 went plowing through the U.S. side of the World Series bracket in Williamsport. They sailed through their three pool-play games. Casey threw a shutout against Phenix City, Alabama, in the first game; a Gaynor hunch paid off in Game 2 when Zack Del Vento, who'd started only once in tournament play, worked more than five innings of a 4–0 shutout of Boise, Idaho; and three pitchers produced a 3–1 victory over Brownsburg, Indiana, that ensured Gaynor's team again would play in the U.S. championship. Around the Williamsport campus of Little League International, the buzz was audible: Japan was steadily advancing again through the International bracket. This team was not from Kashima, but rather Hirakata, near Osaka. But no matter: If it was Toms River against Japan in a rematch for the world title, the game might well be the most-watched in Little League history.

As Gaynor's team cooled its heels and waited, the team from Phenix City got on a roll and played its way back into the U.S. championship game. For Gaynor, that was the good news. The Alabama team had barely touched Casey in that first game, and Gaynor was going to send his son right back out there to take care of the U.S. title and give Toms River a chance to repeat as World Series champions.

And, for one inning, that's exactly what happened. On Thursday evening, August 26, 1999, Casey Gaynor strode to the mound and began firing bullets at the Phenix City batters. His teammates scored two quick first-inning runs, and Casey looked absolutely unhittable. Two runs, for Casey, were probably one more than he would even need.

But that was before the rain.

When the storms moved through the Williamsport area on Thursday, Series officials had a call to make. They could move the Toms River–Phenix City game to a Friday start, or they could roll the dice with the Thursday weather and see if they could sneak in the game. They went for trying to play Thursday, partly to stay on their TV schedule, but they managed to get in only the one inning before the rain made it impossible to continue—disappointing news for the thousands of Toms River fans who had made the drive in time for the evening game, and who then had to turn around and head home for work on Friday.

Now the network, and Little League officials, faced another decision. ESPN had two time slots available for Friday, one at 11 a.m. and the other at 5 p.m. A replay was scheduled for the early slot and an All-Star exhibition game—comprising players whose teams were not in the Series final—was set for the late slot. Officials decided to use the morning spot for the Toms River game.

"It was the biggest mistake they ever made," Mike Gaynor said. "They should have played the All-Star Game at eleven a.m., because nobody was watching anyway, and then, for ratings, the five o'clock game would've been off the charts, with everybody in the East coming home from work."

Instead, the players had to get up the next morning and get ready to go again. And Gaynor had to decide whether to send Casey back to the pitcher's mound.

If Casey's arm was stiff from having warmed up, begun pitching, and then retreating in the rain the night before, then Gaynor would go with Eric Campesi on Friday morning. If Casey felt good and loose, Gaynor would allow him to continue. He didn't have the option to start Eric and then bring in Casey, because this was technically a resumption of play from Thursday night; since Casey had been the starting pitcher, his only choice was either to continue pitching as play began, or come out of the game for good.

"What do you want to do?" Gaynor asked his son. "It's you or Eric."

"I want to go," Casey said.

That was what Gaynor wanted to hear, and so on Friday morning he sent his son to the mound, with all of those shutout innings he had been racking up. But Casey had nothing left. As Gaynor watched Casey's first pitch sail ineffectively over the plate Friday morning, he turned to his friend Ken Kondek near the dugout and said, "He ain't got it." And Gaynor was right: In the bottom of the second inning, Casey suddenly, shockingly yielded a home run to an Alabama player named William Gaston III. It was the first run Casey had allowed in six games. It was the second home run William Gaston had ever hit. And it changed everything. With Casey struggling to get any sort of velocity or break on his pitches, the Phenix City hitters found their confidence, quickly reeled off four straight singles, scored twice more and took a 3–2 lead before Gaynor could replace his son with Eric Campesi. Campesi was brilliant; he proceeded to throw a shutout for the rest of the game. But the damage had been done: the Toms River kids were knocked off stride, and they weren't the world's heaviest-hitting bunch of Little Leaguers anyway. When they began to flail at Alabama pitcher Bryan Woodall's tight-breaking curveball, Gaynor knew his guys were in trouble.

Woodall pitched the game of his life, five shutout innings in relief. Phenix City made the one rally against Casey stand up. The final score was 3–2, a colossal upset. Officials estimated the crowd at Lamade Stadium at about 11,000, less than half the number of people who had been on hand Thursday night before the weather changed the schedule.

Phenix City's victory seemed to take some of the starch out of the '99 World Series. Although the Alabama team was a great story, especially for the players rebounding the way they did against Casey after having been shut out by him in their first game at Williamsport, there was no doubt that America was looking forward to a Toms River–Japan re-match. It wasn't to be.

In the Toms River dugout, several kids quietly cried, their dream evaporated in a surprising twist. Then, at Gaynor's direction, they rose to the top steps of their dugout and applauded the Phenix City team, wishing the players good luck in the Series championship. There was nothing left to do. Had the game been scheduled at five in the afternoon, it was entirely possible that Casey could have worked the stiffness out of his arm by taking a jog and throwing some "long toss," the football-style looping throws that pitchers often make as they loosen up. Neither Gaynor nor Casey would ever know for sure.

As Gaynor slowly made his way out of Lamade Stadium and across the Williamsport campus, most of his players having gone on ahead of him, he was approached by an executive with the ABC network, which would be televising the World Series championship Saturday, now to include Phenix City and Japan.

"He puts his arm around me and he goes like this," Gaynor said, tapping a closed fist lightly against his heart in a pantomime of someone attempting to stab himself. "He goes, 'That killed me.' This is his quote: 'Saturday would have been the greatest sporting event in the history of our country.' It would have been bigger than the World Series, bigger than the Super Bowl. He said the repeat implications of Toms River and Japan, it would have been just off the freaking charts. And I know this: If we had gotten into that game, I don't even know how you would have hosted it in that town. Our championship game crowd on Thursday night, before the rain, was the largest they'd ever had [more than 27,000 people]. We had people following us, because we were the Beast of the East, and we were repeating. You have no idea."

But Gaynor was nothing if not a realist when it came to baseball, his players and their limits. He believed that if the Phenix City game had been played continuously, either Thursday night or from start to finish on Friday, then Casey likely would have thrown a shutout and gotten Toms River East back to the World Series championship. And Gaynor also believed that Japan would have destroyed his proud, overachieving bunch.

"I've been down the road long enough," Gaynor said. "I know sometimes what it feels like when you're over-matched, and I had seen Japan's ace pitcher, and he was pretty special, pretty special. We weren't going to get to that kid, and I would have used Casey already just to pitch us to that point, to even reach that game. We weren't star-studded. We were not loaded by any means. And I'll go on the record: If we had played that Japan team in the final in '99, we're not winning."

He paused. "But I sure would have loved that game."

As it was, Japan's ace, Kazuki Sumiyama, struck out nine Alabama hitters on Saturday en route to a 5–0 shutout that returned the Little League World Championship to Japan after a one-year stay near the Jersey Shore. Mike Gaynor and his kids returned home to a warm welcome, ribbons and streamers placed around the East Little League complex—and a message from the producers of the *Regis and Kathie Lee* television show, which already had inquired about the boys making the trip to New York to appear on an upcoming telecast.

The message: Maybe next year. We'll be in touch.

The loss in '99, the sort of bittersweet and quite possibly avoidable defeat at the hands of another U.S. team, actually served to heighten the Toms River profile. The talk of how the gods had conspired to ruin a potential repeat kept the Beast of the East in the chatter for months, long after Mike Gaynor, with his son Casey now finished at the Little League level, had retired as a coach and gone back to running the athletic shoe stores he owned in the area. In time, Gaynor would trade out that part of his life, too, spending a couple of years coaching at the high school level and eventually remaking himself as a real estate broker.

But the Little League image wasn't going away just because the Gaynor family was done; nor would it be unwound by the fact that there were no Frazier stars left to come blasting through the rosters. The image continued to define, and occasionally bedevil, Toms River from that moment on. When the boys from Toms River American Little League reached the regional final in Bristol in the summer of 2005, it was taken more as simple confirmation that the town was still a baseball juggernaut than anything else. It didn't matter if, upon reflection, the Mike Gaynor years might actually be understood as a brilliant fluke. For that matter, people outside the district wouldn't distinguish between Gaynor's run of three World Series teams in five years and Toms River American's near-miss in 2005. To most folks, it was all the same.

They heard "Toms River," and that was enough. Toms River was now, officially, a factory town. What it produced was ballplayers.

BY THE SUMMER OF 2007, it was difficult to fathom that Toms River had ever been anything but a baseball town. In scope, ambition and growth, the facilities at both Little League complexes were extraordinary. The East location off Windsor, while no thing of beauty, clearly displayed the fruits of all of its winning. In the wake of the '98 World Series title and '99 appearance, league officials launched a fund-raising effort to expand the number of fields from

seven to nine. Rosie O'Donnell, who had Gaynor's victori-
ous 1998 group as guests on her TV show, chipped in with
a pitching machine, which was installed inside a new, year-
round indoor training center in the middle of the complex.
League officials collected $185,000 in private contributions
to help build it; it had three batting cages, fluorescent overhead lighting, a video setup to better evaluate batters' swings
and pitchers' motions, and two walls' worth of trophy cases
to hold all the plaques and newspaper articles, framed photos and assorted memorabilia that came flooding in while
Gaynor's teams were storming Williamsport.

From the time that Gaynor's first squad made it to the
Series in 1995, the local competition began to heat up—
even the competition for facilities. East, after all, was technically the second league in town, the one that had been spun
off from Toms River Little League in the 1960s, several years
after the original league had been chartered with four teams.
The Mapletree complex was the first significant youth baseball structure built in the town, yet the trips to the World
Series had changed everything. Suddenly, Toms River East
was the league that the locals associated with quality and
excellence. "And they didn't let anyone forget it," one TRLL
parent noted.

In the years that followed, though, a gradual but per-
ceptible shift began to occur, as the glory of those teams of
the '90s began to fade slightly and demographics and money
forced new ways of thinking about the division of young
baseball talent in town. Probably the most astonishing development, and ultimately the most significant, came in 1999.
The same year that Gaynor made it three World Series ap-

pearances in five years, Toms River Little League received a $500,000 grant from the state of New Jersey to begin aggressively upgrading its Mapletree layout. Combined with a loan, the money enabled the league to build a year-round practice facility and to finish its eight fields, from tee-ball all the way through to the senior leagues. Toms River Little League may not have had banners, but it had momentum—and an increasing share of the baseball population, as building patterns shifted and new construction popped up farther and farther west of Hooper Avenue. By 2005 it was TRLL, not TRELL, that sponsored a slight majority of the nearly 2,000 young ballplayers in town, a number that works out to more than 2 percent of Toms River's total population.

The rivalry had grown along with the rest of it. What Gaynor's teams accomplished was first received as a miraculous stroke of fortune for the town; but given time and the usual patterns of jealousy and competitiveness that veered from good-natured to overtly hostile and back again depending on the day, there came a point at which the folks from Toms River Little League didn't want to hear about it anymore. When someone mentioned the impressive collection of signs at the East complex, a parent of one of John Puleo's players curtly replied, "They may need to touch those up a little bit"—a biting reference to the fact that, since the final World Series entry of '99, Toms River East had been unable to replicate its success. The signs were beginning to show their age.

For their part, East coaches and parents could take solace in the fact that their league was still the ultimate expression of Little League in the area. "We haven't had that much good news around here in recent years," said one coach, "but everybody knows the history. Believe me, everybody knows the history. They sure know it over there on Mapletree."

Among adults, it sometimes seemed that only Mike Gaynor truly understood what a wicked lightning strike of luck it had all been. His All-Star teams were indisputably good, but also very lucky. There was no better way to explain how even a very talented roster could play its way through a 2,400-team snake pit like the Eastern Region one time, much less do it three times.

Gaynor certainly didn't become a shadow figure in the years following the great triumphs of his Little League teams; he was seldom afraid to remind anyone of the enormous odds his teams had overcome—and of the notion that with three winners in five years, the only real constant was Gaynor himself. Yet when Gaynor referred to each leg of his teams' Williamsport runs as being "like hitting the lottery," he wasn't being entirely self-deprecating.

Still, the World Series appearances spoke to more than luck. "I don't want to sound like a jerk, but I've seen better teams than mine even in our own local Little League," Gaynor said, the implication being that those teams simply got outcoached. Gaynor relished his own role in the history, and he never apologized for the subsequent fame, neither his nor his players'. The annual summertime collection of Mike Gaynor All-Star Baseball Camps, an almost constant reminder of his teams' achievements, attested to that.

But Gaynor could see that the town around him had been changed by its baseball success. What it had become by 2007, the year John Puleo and his kids began their own journey, felt far removed from the way things had come about in the 1990s, with their combinations of the right players, coaches, involved parents and healthy ambition. It wasn't that Gaynor's East teams didn't care whether they won, but there was no template for the kind of success they eventually enjoyed. If they lost, they simply lost. There was no weight of history, certainly none any heavier than other towns with Little League dreams might experience. And even after the boys reached Williamsport the first time, in 1995, there was no special suggestion that it should, or even could, happen again. There was a reason you could scroll through the Little League World Series rosters over the years and see so few repeat entries. It was basically a one-shot deal for almost any town lucky enough to ever see it at all.

Gaynor and his coaches went through three trips to the World Series and barely ever mentioned the word Williamsport. "That's too heavy to put on twelve-year-olds," he said. "You just can't go that route. In '98, '99, we never said it. We never used the *W*-word. Our whole approach was, 'Who's our next pitcher?' It was literally one thing at a time." But Gaynor wasn't kidding himself about the changes in Toms River that all the success had produced, and chief among the changes was the newfound expectation of winning—or, more specifically, of winning it all. It was an odd thing to ask a kid to carry around, the hopes of a town.

He rarely said so for the record, but Gaynor had come to agree with a local baseball official, a friend of his, that the Toms River East teams that went to the World Series represented "the best thing that could have happened to us—and the worst." It was the emotional fallout to which his friend was referring. And Gaynor wanted to tell people about that, so it might take some of the edge off the growing pressure in town. Gaynor sometimes saw Toms River's two Little Leagues locked in a sort of grim struggle to produce the next great chapter in the baseball story, and what he knew for certain was that success of the kind his teams enjoyed was awfully hard to force.

The success was, in some ways, the product of a system of baseball that was put in place years before Gaynor arrived on the Little League scene. It was a top-down proposition that now worked two ways: The Little Leagues fed the high school programs, yes; but in the beginning, it was the high school coaches who showed Little League the way to play ball.

WHEN KENNY FRANK ARRIVED IN Toms River near the end of 1969, there was one high school, one baseball field and a quarry's worth of rocks in the infield dirt between first and third base. There were no outfield fences. Instead of a dugout, the Toms River team sat on a bench that had been placed under a shade tree when it was time to take a break, and on game days the squad used a local elementary school field because it was better than what the high school had. There was no inkling that baseball was king.

But the sport became king not long after, in large measure because Frank arrived. Frank, who grew up in Jersey City, had played high school, college and semipro ball, and in '69, as a student teacher, he was quickly hired by Al Fantuzzi to coach the junior varsity baseball team. By 1977, Fantuzzi had moved on, and Frank took over the full program at the school that eventually was renamed Toms River South.

From the start, Frank knew what he wanted to do. His practices became notorious for their rigor and discipline. He ordered his players to run on and off the field at all times, an almost military approach to such a basic task as going out to their positions. He emphasized repetition of form, often having his players put in hundreds of swings in a single day in an effort to develop a batting stance and stroke that could be depended on from one game to the next. He put in a system of signs that he still uses today, nearly 40 years later. He organized Rock Days, so named because the baseball players would spend the day picking the rocks out of the infield dirt. He remade the high school field almost from scratch; it's now known as Ken Frank Field. He forged relationships with the local Little Leagues early on, hosting special game days in their honor. He and Fantuzzi put together instructional camps at Ocean County College that drew not only young players but prospects who might eventually attend High School South, as it was often called, and play baseball the Ken Frank way, disciplined and hustling.

Like Gaynor decades after him, Frank was a patient but utterly firm teacher. His style of play was classic small-ball, with every one of his hitters capable of dropping down a perfect bunt and taking the extra base on a routine hit. The Toms River South Indians sprinted to their positions in the field, and they sprinted off the field when an inning had ended. They emphasized pitching and defense first, figuring they could squeeze across a run or two somehow and make that stand up for the win. In the dugout, they were loud, constant and chirpy with their chatter, and as the years went by and the championships piled up, 20-win seasons became the norm. The bar had been set, and it was sky-high.

In Frank's fourth year as head coach, in 1980, the program went 24–7 and broke through to win the Ocean County championship, and it never looked back. By 2007, Frank's teams had won more than 600 games and captured five New Jersey state titles, and Frank had been selected Ocean County coach of the year 10 times.

Beyond the team's success, though, Frank spawned a baseball passion in the area and, almost unintentionally, created some of the greatest sports rivalries in the area's history. A few years after he became head coach, Frank asked his brother, Bill, and a good friend, Ted Schelmay, to work as his assistants. By the mid-1980s, Bill Frank was the head coach at the new Toms River High School East; a few years after that, Schelmay was hired to take over the program at Toms River North. The three programs mirrored one another in their intense competitiveness and their coaches' insistence on doing the little things right. The success came flowing in, with all three teams routinely listed among New Jersey's top-10 high school programs. The sport had caught fire in Toms River.

"Ken Frank pretty much established the baseball mentality around here a long time ago," said Jack Daubert, the man who built the Hit Dogs training facility. "And, you know, his brother and Ted Schelmay spun off to the other two schools, so the philosophy was set. And when those schools go out to play each other, you just can't believe it."

Frank and his brother find themselves coaching against

each other at least twice every spring, during their teams' regular-season schedules, and they compete mercilessly for victories. The coaches went so hard at it over the years, in fact, that Kenny and Billy eventually struck an agreement that after every South-versus-East game, the brothers would go together for a drink regardless of the outcome. Meanwhile, Schelmay, at North, combined his hard-nosed baseball sense with the choicest demographics of the rapidly growing Toms River area.

As word grew of the year-in, year-out quality of all three programs, the town's interest followed right along. Suddenly, the unprecedented became routine: When two of Toms River's high school teams played each other in baseball, crowds of 2,000 and even 3,000 people would show up—many more than the scant handfuls of fans who usually come to see their high school and college teams play.

"Thousands of people," Kenny Frank said one morning, cozied into a booth at a local diner, where he was interrupted several times by people who wanted to say hello or tell him about a player they had coming up through the system who might be South bound in a few years. "The competitive nature of these programs and the parents— you can't believe it. When we play each other, they take days off from work to be at those games. Watch one of the high school games, and you'll be able to understand everything that anybody has ever told you about the sport in Toms River."

Frank's winning habits created the template for success with baseball, and since Toms River didn't have a reputation in sports at the time, baseball became it. Over time, baseball at the Little League level was identified as the natural precursor to all of that high school success. The kids needed to be ready to learn how to win when they were young, because there was no way they could arrive at one of the high school programs and compete for a spot unless they had the winning mentality already locked in place.

In every way, Kenny Frank did what he could to establish and then maintain the connection between Little League and the high schools. Even now, he said, "the Little Leagues come in droves to our games, because a lot of their coaches are the people who coached our varsity players back when they were in Little League themselves. The coaches feel like they've had a big part in developing them, which they have."

The Frank family also knew Mike Gaynor well: Bill's son, Brad Frank, was a member of Gaynor's 1998 World Series champions. Kenny Frank followed that team all the way to Williamsport to watch his nephew compete. Toms River's victory over Japan, Kenny said, ranked as one of his peak experiences in the sport, though he was but a spectator.

But Kenny Frank also saw that the victory, and its attendant publicity, had changed things in Toms River. And the changes he was seeing, especially the more recent ones, were not necessarily for the better.

"Ever since Mike took that team to the championship, if you win the districts in Little League anymore, it's like, 'Oh, you only won the district,'" Frank said. "And winning the district around here is very tough—very tough. College scouts, college coaches like kids from this New Jersey area because they're tough kids. We rake our own fields, and we have to get everything ready to play a game. Tough kids. Are they better than California kids? Probably not. Better than Florida kids? Probably not. But they play because they really want to play."

What Frank had noticed more specifically in recent years was the increasing tendency of parents to chase travel-team dreams, often at the expense of Little League. "It used to be that everybody played Little League," he said. "But they're starting to tell the kids to play travel ball and not Little League, and I think they might get burned out too early. Little League has been successful here. The kids have come from Little League and then worked their way through the intermediate level to the high school. Now I've got guys who have six-year-olds saying, 'Have you got somebody to work with him on his hitting?' Come on: I'd just be taking his money at that point, because the kid doesn't have the hand-eye coordination at that age to be working on hitting like that. Send him to the camps, let him get a little camaraderie with the other kids. Then, as they grow, they're a part of something, and I think that's what makes it work."

"Just growing up around here, you hear it all the time: The Toms River teams, their success," said Charlie Frazier, who played for Kenny Frank at High School South and now is one of his assistant coaches. "I'm happy that these kids work this hard and want it so bad, but some of them don't realize that it's a whole team thing. You've got to have the right caliber people, the right pitching—you have to have all kinds of power to do it. It's a good feeling to know that the town is competitive and wants to get back to Williamsport, but, you know, you've got to understand that at Little League baseball, they're trying to develop themselves to get to be on the high school team."

Clearly, by 2007, some parents no longer considered that track fast enough. They still valued Little League; they still interpreted their children's baseball dreams—and their own dreams for their children—as leading to Williamsport at age 12. But they did not agree that Little League alone offered enough practice, experience or coaching to get their kids to the next level. If they believed that, there would be no reason for a place like Hit Dogs to exist.

ABOUT 200 YARDS NORTH OF the exit onto Industrial Way, just off State Route 37, sits an unremarkable building on an unremarkable piece of land in an area optimistically dubbed Toms River Corporate Park. There is no hint of the hum of activity inside.

To look at the 9,000-square-foot spread, and at the state-of-the-art baseball and weight-training equipment, it could be hard to accept that the Hit Dogs Sports Training Facility, as it is fancifully known, began in the basement of Jack Daubert's home in 2000. Daubert, a lifelong baseball fanatic who, like John Puleo, had grown up in the northern New Jersey town of Bloomfield, was the father of baseball-playing sons in Toms River. He found himself looking for a place for them and their friends to get some swings during the snowy, cold months, and lacking any better alternative he built a cage in the basement of his house. His sons and friends like Charlie Frazier, whose brothers both had been stars on Mike Gaynor's World Series teams, began spending hours and hours down there. One thing led to another, friend told friend, and the practice space became a raucous daily ritual for dozens of kids. Pretty soon Daubert's wife told Jack, "You'd better do something about this."

So Jack moved the cage out. His first venture landed him in a building just across Route 37 from where he eventually moved; his initial space was a modest and affordable 1,600 square feet; his coaching staff consisted primarily of his sons, Jake and Luke, and Charlie Frazier; and his goal was simply to pay the rent each month. What Jack hadn't counted on was the almost manic fallout of the Little League World Series years in Toms River and the numbers of kids that this success had driven into the arms of youth baseball. He had built the right facility at exactly the right time.

Once word got out about Hit Dogs, finding a reason to go there was easy for legions of Toms River kids and their parents. Charlie Frazier, after all, not only had been a local high school star, but he went on to be drafted by the Florida Marlins and played five years in the minor leagues. Jake Daubert earned a full scholarship to play baseball at Rutgers, then was drafted by the Seattle Mariners, and was still playing ball in the independent leagues now and again. As time went on, Hit Dogs got occasional instructors like Jeff Frazier, who was by then a star at Rutgers and got drafted by the Detroit Tigers—and, just as noteworthy for Toms River, had been the star of the '95 Little League World Series team. The business grew more and more popular, forcing Jack Daubert to move into the new, larger space, with its new, larger rent payment.

Hit Dogs was a baseball fanatic's paradise. The facility featured a full weight room, hitting and pitching stations, and fielding areas. You could have a team there and be working at three or four different stations constantly. A team could get a full-throttle workout in under an hour, rain or shine, in January or June.

John Puleo's decision to get his returning All-Stars in there over the winter of 2006–7 wasn't particularly surprising to Daubert and his crew. They had been seeing more and more of that kind of year-round approach to the game, with kids—or their parents—insisting upon never letting that swing get rusty, or never letting the pitching arm fall out of shape. There no longer was an excuse to take a season off. You could do your baseball work all year long. And considering that the other towns were probably doing so, on some level you couldn't afford not to keep up.

At the same time, Daubert was experiencing a paradigm shift in his clientele. From its inception in his basement, the Hit Dogs approach was primarily created with the competitive player in mind, kids who were going for coveted spots on the local high school teams. Toms River had gotten into the habit of producing so many good young players that there wasn't room for all of them even among the three varsity programs in town. Players, and their parents, felt they had to either raise their games or concede their roster spots. Hit Dogs had a built-in, renewable base of business.

But now Daubert was seeing something else entirely: By the summer of 2007, his fastest-growing demographic among paying customers was the six-and-under set. Hit Dogs was growing younger, so much younger that it sometimes resembled a day-care facility as much as a place to learn baseball. Around the building, kindergartners romped on the artificial turf or played made-up games of pitch and catch by the nets. Parents jammed their young children into hitting sessions or weeklong day-camps that were focused entirely on teaching the basic skills the tots would need to succeed in Little League.

John Puleo's interest in Hit Dogs was only slightly less grandiose. He saw in its climate-controlled shelter the perfect way to remind his players over the winter that they were, first and foremost, part of an elite collection that could be something great in 2007. It wasn't healthy to have all that time off and never think about baseball. They'd never get the edge back if they put it aside completely. They had to keep a hand in it somehow. And John wouldn't rest easy unless he had done everything he could do about that.

So the winter became notable for the weekend sessions at the facility, with actual baseball skills playing a relatively minor role. By December, John had ordered the kids to put down the bats and balls, and not to pick them up again until February. He wanted the team together, but not necessarily to pitch their way through the cold months. Instead, John hired the services of a strength-and-conditioning coach, and once every Saturday the coach put the young athletes to the test, working on their agility, their fitness and their core strength. John didn't care about the particulars so much; he just wanted the group together. And despite the other things competing for their time—basketball, hockey, wrestling and the like—attendance was almost always excellent.

For Hit Dogs, it was just another team session, of which plenty were scheduled over the months. The real money lay in private and small-group lessons, where the kids were being brought in to work on a swing or develop a pitch. By the summer of '07, Hit Dogs was getting seventy dollars an hour for individual lessons, and it was almost scheduled out. Jack Daubert's e-mail list alone, which was compiled strictly of the addresses of people who had already visited the facility, was at 1,100 and rising.

"I remember playing in Little League, and playing in the minors, and mostly just having fun," said Jonathan Pauciullo, a 19-year-old instructor at Hit Dogs. "I hear now from some of my kids that their minor-league teams are practicing four hours a day, two sessions. Two-a-days! That's incredible. They're twelve. Four hours a day they work. Four hours? You could've played two whole games in four hours."

Then again, Pauciullo grew up in Toms River, and "I've had a ball and bat in my hands since I was three. A lot of us have. The baseball was always good here, even before the Little League thing. The Little League stuff just made it that much bigger."

"I will tell you a story," the ruddy-faced Daubert said one day, seated in his office behind a standard-issue business desk that looked like it could barely contain his large frame and thick arms. Baseball books and instructional videos were strewn around the desk and throughout the room, including the workspace occupied by Charlie Frazier, who gave lessons at Hit Dogs in between his teaching job at Toms River North High School and his work as one of Kenny Frank's coaches at Toms River South.

Daubert went on to say that he had received a call the week before, from the man who wanted to get his son some hitting instruction. Daubert asked a little about the boy, and the father quickly rattled off some impressive statistics from the season before, when he said his son had batted over .500, with an even higher on-base percentage. The man felt that the player had a good swing but a few mechanical flaws in it, and he was sure that some lessons at Hit Dogs could iron out the kinks.

Jack finally asked how old the man's son was.

"He's five," the father replied.

"So . . . he was in tee-ball last season?" Daubert asked.

"Yeah."

"Wait: You kept stats on your son's tee-ball season?"

"Yeah!" the man replied—according to Daubert, without the slightest hint of embarrassment.

It was not a unique conversation. In fact, such interactions almost certainly are the future of Hit Dogs. The place glows with the finely honed expectations of the parents who bring their very young sons and daughters there, either for baseball or softball instruction. Daubert and his staff, over the past couple of years, found themselves increasingly answering questions that once would have seemed either quaint or downright foolish, sometimes being asked to guess the career trajectory of an athlete who hadn't yet hit double digits in age.

"We've had parents come in here with nine-year-olds, wanting them to be taught curveballs so they can succeed in some nine-year-old tournament," Jack said. "We won't do that. It's crazy. But you have to understand the mentality. I've had guys come in here and tell me that their kid is going to get a Division One scholarship, and the kid is ten years old.

"That's the thinking here. 'We're going to go to Williamsport every year,' is the thinking. People look right past the district now. They're going to Williamsport."

Charlie Frazier, seated at the other desk, looking over some paperwork, suddenly sat forward in his chair and smiled.

"But we love it," Frazier said.

"Absolutely. We love it," Daubert said. "But at the same time, they're kids. Ever since the Little League thing in the nineties, we've seen more and more scouts in the area, and sometimes they'll scout the kids at a very early age. By the time they get to high school and American Legion ball, they've been scouted quite a bit. This has become a highly recruited area, in part because of the Little League success and all that."

The Little League adventures had, in truth, brought attention of every sort, and on a scale that the town sometimes found difficult to manage. It also exposed Toms River—and some of its baseball families—to the dark side of celebrity.

In 2003, camera crews arrived in the city to gather the raw footage that eventually became Toms River's most profoundly embarrassing baseball moment: a two-night special on ESPN that was part of the network's *The Season* series. For weeks and weeks that summer, coaches and parents granted the crews access to Toms River East Little League, from board meetings to dugout conversations and mound conferences. The idea, at first, was to put together an inside look at the daily life of a truly competitive Little League. The parents and coaches at East felt that ESPN had come to the right place. After all, they had never been afraid of their own competitive nature; to them, it was part of the world in which they lived. Where else would ESPN go? Toms River East was surely the destination, given its recent history. In the beginning of the filming, the East coaches and families felt honored.

The resulting program, culled from those endless hours of videotape, was so mortifying to the league that after the first night, several parents said they prayed the second night's install- ment might somehow get knocked off the air. Film footage made with the full consent of the league showed parents in angry arguments with one another, kids crying on the pitcher's mound, board members sipping beers as they debated All-Star team selections, coaches screaming at preteen players, manag- ers sneaking cigarettes between innings in back of the dugout. It was raw, and it was remarkably unflattering. Taken together, the images conveyed the unmistakable impression of a place that had spun out of control. While people outside of town saw the show as a reasonable attempt to document a complicated, emotional sacred cow like youth baseball, many Toms River families interpreted it as a broadside attack on the local league, a sort of video chronicle of lost values and parental ambition that superseded all other considerations.

"They cut out every decent thing we ever did," one parent said years later, still seething at the recollections. "It was the worst rip job you ever saw. It was almost like Toms River was riding too high, and there had to be something wrong so they could take us down."

Mike Gaynor, who spent both nights of the presenta- tion squirming in his chair, afraid that some part of the in- terview he had given ESPN for the program might air (it didn't), felt bad for a different reason.

"The sad part of it is, that stuff did actually go on," Gaynor said. "It didn't happen when I was coaching, and I had never seen anything like it—but obviously it did go on, because it was right there on film. You couldn't argue with that. Sure, they might have taken the worst parts and put them in the show, but we had to look at the fact that those parts did happen, or else they couldn't have been included. And it traveled, too. My guys down in Cape May and Atlantic County were calling me, asking, 'Does this really go on in your league?' And I didn't know what to say. I mean, evidently so.

"It was unbelievable how that show tore this town apart. It was about the pressure we put on our kids, everything that's wrong with Little League. It was about the pressure to play every year at that level."

At the World Series level, Gaynor meant—and funny that he should say it. In the three visits Gaynor and his Little League teams had made to Williamsport, not once had a kid blown apart or a parent fallen into screaming spasms. Maybe Gaynor had all the good kids. Maybe he knew what he was doing when he set the tone for the workouts and game situations. Maybe it had something to do with the fact that, to Gaynor, the idea of "expecting" to win some grand prize seemed almost comically at odds with reality. He and his coaches had fended off that mind-set as much as they could—even if, in reality, the kids surely knew what the goals were. Some pressure was not only unavoidable, but natural. Why bother to keep score otherwise?

◆ ◆ ◆

IN THE END, GAYNOR'S EXPERIENCE had taught him that it was hard to win with a 900-pound gorilla on your back, even for the Beast of the East. In the summer of 2007, he looked across town and saw John Puleo and his guys beginning to shoulder that weight, and Gaynor thought he understood. It was no longer easy, being from Toms River. The great players just embraced that notion and kept on punching forward. Gaynor hoped that John had enough of the great ones.

CHAPTER 3

SUMMER OF POSSIBILITIES

"ALL RIGHT, THEN," COACH JOHN said. "Everybody give me ten."

Amid the groans and the ribbing, most of it directed semigleefully at Johnny, the boys of Toms River American did as they were told. Bending and kneeling down to the grass of the practice field at the Mapletree complex, they dutifully squeezed off 10 push-ups, counting them out as a team—"One! Two! Three! Four!"—as they'd been taught to do the summer before. It was business as usual. Johnny had gone and ticked off his dad again.

From Matt Volk's perspective, the push-ups officially made this an All-Star practice. Matt, who usually went by the nickname "Mo," had logged plenty of time with both of the Puleos over the past two years, being a member of John's Red Sox team during the Little League regular season and these stints with the All-Star squads. He had seen the father-son dynamic at work for months, and Mo knew this much: Johnny Puleo could be counted on at least once each workout session, and quite often more than once, to either say or do something that cost his team push-ups.

Sometimes, like today, it could just as easily be a matter of what Johnny *didn't* do. Moments earlier, Mo hit a grounder to the left side of the infield during batting practice. Johnny, playing shortstop, had conspicuously failed to charge the ball, which rolled to a near stop on the infield grass. By the time Johnny picked it up and lobbed a casual, after-the-fact throw to first, Mo was well across the bag with a single.

"Stop! Stop! Stop!" an exasperated Coach John barked. Then, approaching his son, he said, "Why didn't you attack that ball?"

"I figured the third baseman would get it," Johnny shot back, quietly but clearly.

"You what?"

"Third baseman's ball," Johnny repeated—an assertion this time, not an explanation.

This just in: push-ups all around.

By the end of the summer of 2007, John Puleo was almost going to need to send his son a thank-you note for his contribution to improving the overall strength of the American All-Stars. With Johnny finding a daily way to get under his dad's skin, those push-ups would become as routine a part of the practice schedule as bunt coverages and outfield flies. Here in June, with the first game of district play less than two weeks away, Coach John couldn't tolerate any dissent, least of all from his son; and Johnny was a talker, especially when it came to questioning or needling his dad. Of course, John could order the push-ups as the result of any number of other things, and from anyone on the team: botched coverages; failures to pick up the signs the coach was giving; lack of hustle from practice drill to practice drill. Sometimes the exercise was simply a wake-up call when John felt the kids hadn't come to the field prepared or energized.

In general, though, Johnny led the pack. "No one else ever has to take the rap for us doing all those push-ups," the coach said, watching his players give him 10. "Johnny always makes sure we get 'em done right in the middle of practice—ten at a time."

It was probably easier that way. In some important aspects of the team dynamic, it was better for the coach to drop the hammer on his own son than on another member of the roster. For John to be willing to discipline Johnny—or, to discipline the entire team on Johnny's behalf—sent a message to the other kids that, for as long as they were at the complex, the focus was to be on baseball and on getting things done. And, of course, Johnny made it easy sometimes. A genuine competitor who in almost every other way was a willing and compliant worker, Johnny often couldn't help himself when it came to defying his dad, whether it was questioning the routine of the practice, deflecting small-time blame from a blown play, or simply wondering aloud why in the world Coach John was asking the kids to work on a particular drill.

"So we all do ten push-ups," Mo said. "And the funny thing is, Johnny never really learns. It seems like we wind up doing these same push-ups all the time."

But the larger truth was that Johnny Puleo's transgressions were the slightest of the slight, and both he and his father knew it—and that knowledge was precisely why they could weather whatever happened on the practice field. It wasn't easy being the coach's son. To be the son of the coach—any coach, not just John—almost always meant hewing to a different standard of performance. John knew full well that he was harder on Johnny than on anyone else on the team that he was less willing to entertain dissent or back talk from Johnny than from, say, Vinny or Quintin or one of the other fun-loving but chirpy members of the squad. When one of those players blew a coverage or kicked up a fuss, John's usual response was to fall back into his patient, good-guy approach to coaching—laughing along with their jokes, accepting a little teasing or grousing about a workout. It was easier for John in those situations to take it for what it was: mostly harmless chatter coming from the kids with whom he had enjoyed such a great run in the summer of 2006, with whom he had forged a real bond, in whom he trusted to snap to it when the time really called for that. It was as though, in his eyes, the guys had earned the right to clown around a little.

With Johnny, though, the coach had little tolerance. It was a purely human response to the ordinary strain of the situation. John was trying to control an entire group of 12- and 13-year-old players that had a serious goal in mind, and the thing he felt the least like dealing with was back talk from his own son. That part, of course, put John in the company of 99.9 percent of the other parents in history who'd ever tried to coach their own children—and it certainly was par for the course in an all-volunteer setup like Little League.

Little League, the world's largest youth sports organization whose annual international participation numbers close to 3 million kids, essentially stands on the shoulders of people like John and Diane Puleo, and John's assistants Jerry Volk, Paul Fabricatore and Scott Ringel. They are the adults who give their time and talent, do most of the heavy lifting, take care of the scheduling, do the driving and the packing and the unpacking and the cleanup, who willingly and actively lose money on the deal—all in the service of their kids and a notion of what the sport can be if the right folks get behind it and push hard. Without such people, the organization would fall apart in less time than it takes to play six innings of kid baseball, and that goes all the way up and down the chain of command in any of the local organizing bodies that make up Little League as a whole. As John was always quick to point out, the guy in the oversized baseball cap quietly sweeping the trash away from the concession area at Mapletree was no maintenance worker; it was Joe Cudia, president of Toms River Little League, whose own son had long since graduated out of the youth baseball system and who kept coming back, year after year, to serve. Even the umpires in Williamsport, the competitive apex of the organization, are volunteers; they pay their own way to be there and officiate the games.

The system is never perfect, and it is always messy, especially on the coaching level. For all the mothers and fathers who prove to be adept at interacting with and instructing groups of young children, there are stories of another breed, from coaches who are just plain unhelpful, to the fringe extremes who, from appearances, lose their bearings completely every time they find themselves in the middle of an actual game, crippled by their inability to control their competitive instincts. It's a common scene anywhere youth baseball is played: the coach screaming at his team in the middle of a game, who flies off the handle at a botched call by one of the volunteer umps who are also part and parcel of the Little League experience.

John, an upbeat man both by habit and by determination, had long been hailed as a person who knew how to coach and deal effectively—and enthusiastically—with young players. More to the point, he had earned the trust of the American All-Stars and their parents because of the successes of the year before. The whole experience had been one giant ferris-wheel ride; everyone walked away happy. But despite that, John never strayed too far from his basic concerns: fun and family. This was especially true when it came to his kids. John keenly felt the need to strike a balance with Johnny. Sitting at a kitchen table in the Puleo family home one evening, he suddenly said to a fellow Little League parent, "You're a coach and you're a father. What's your fear? That you'll do harm to your kid and drive him away from enjoying the game, right? Well, that's my fear, too."

"I don't want to do harm," John said, "so if I get into an argument with Johnny on the baseball field, I feel fifty times worse afterward, because I'm thinking to myself, 'Did I do harm to this boy? Am I driving him away from something that should be fun? Am I expecting too much from him because of the family he's from?'"

John constantly ran such thoughts through his mind, which helped to explain why he was such a good Little League coach, and so valued. He genuinely cared, and not only about his son. John was no saint; he wanted to win as badly as anyone in Toms River. He had the ego to believe he could coach a team all the way to Williamsport, the odds be hanged, and he wanted to be the person who brought the newspaper headlines back to town once more. He wouldn't waste a minute pretending otherwise, because John did not consider such a goal to be anything but worthy and healthy. He believed completely in the value of competition. He certainly wasn't afraid to be ambitious. It was his idea, after all, to bring the Williamsport photo to practice.

But John also had the ability to step back, and he tried to do so every day. The coach always seemed aware that the mini-cosmos of kid baseball was a world within the real world. It was a game that could teach life lessons, but a game all the same.

John, too, knew who he was. He knew from whence he came. And he never forgot it—for his own sake and for Johnny's.

Like so many others he knew in Toms River, John had grown up somewhere else, in Bloomfield, 70 miles to the north. "I grew up in a neighborhood where, when you stick your hand out the window of your house, you hit another house," he said one day. "See this grass? We had no grass." He grew up not far from Jack Daubert, the Hit Dogs founder. Daubert knew the Puleo family. How could he not? John's brother Charlie Puleo was part of that clan, and everybody knew Charlie.

Charlie Puleo was, as baseballers like to say about one another, a *player*. He was the real deal. A high school star who just kept going, Charlie made it all the way to the big leagues, spending eight seasons with the New York Mets, the Cincinnati Reds and the Atlanta Braves—this despite the fact, John says, that the boys' father seldom played catch with them when they were growing up, because of his heavy workload. Charlie made it anyway. He was a hero to the family, the guy with all the athletic prowess who actually made his dreams come true. He is recalled in baseball history mostly as a footnote, as the player who was traded for Tom Seaver when Seaver returned to the Mets before the 1983 season; but within his extended family and his Bloomfield hometown, Charlie was the one who went all the way to the Show. He pitched in eight different big-league seasons during the 1980s. He hit a home run—him, a pitcher!—off the Cubs' Rick Sutcliffe, during a game at Wrigley Field in the spring of 1987. It was an almost impossible dream, all of it.

Now John, who loved baseball and played on a Division Three World Series entrant at Upsala College, sometimes felt concerned that Johnny might carry the weight of Uncle Charlie's accomplishments. Deep down, he knew that Johnny wanted success for himself, not to prove anything to anyone else in the Puleo clan, but still there was no question that Johnny knew all the stories about Charlie. The pressure he felt was not unlike that of the Toms River Little Leaguers, with their connection to the town's World Series history. In both cases, the pressure was real no matter how it was created.

Really, though, John needn't have worried much. He was the father of a player who, despite generally betraying little emotion on the field during games, burned inside the way the true competitors do. Johnny didn't spend much time thinking about the family legacy; he was too busy trying to get his game to the elite level so Toms River American could bop its way out of the state tournament, on through regionals, and straight ahead to Williamsport.

Johnny was an infant when Toms River East Little League first went to the World Series in 1995, and he hadn't even begun tee-ball by the time Mike Gaynor's kids won it all in 1998. The stories to him were more legend than reality; he understood that all this had happened, but, as he put it, "I think it's something that means more to the parents than it does to me." All Johnny knew was that there wasn't anything keeping a Toms River team from going all the way. The titles didn't have to go to some richer place, or some place with deeper talent or cooler uniforms.

Johnny found himself on the cusp of great change in the summer of 2007. He was a boy transitioning through adolescence, not far away now from being a young man. He had just completed sixth grade, having spent his year trying to get into the flow of life at Toms River North Intermediate School, which he would attend until ninth grade. Like most of his friends, he'd swing back and forth between goofily mastering Guitar Hero on his PlayStation and growling like a grown-up when things didn't go right on the baseball diamond. He was a good student who stayed out of trouble, the oldest of three children, a kid—like many of the kids among the Toms River Americans—who was grounded by a stable, traditional family structure, in a city of 90,000 that was almost exclusively white and substantially middle class. The Toms River American All-Stars mostly lived in four-bedroom houses on roomy lots with nice yards, part of a low-crime community that, even with its proximity to the Shore, had stayed affordable for long enough that it was not surprising for a family to have a good-sized place to call home.

And baseball was the binding that held much of his life together. Johnny had been playing ball since he could remember. His dad had been his coach from the minute Johnny stepped onto a field at the Mapletree complex. He had taken up other sports and liked them, basketball in particular; but when it came to choosing, there wasn't really a close second. Johnny played baseball first, foremost and with a substantial portion of his self-identity attached.

Johnny particularly didn't care about the leagues. Toms River East represented to him another couple of teams his squad might need to beat in the district tournament. The rivalry between the leagues was felt by the adults and coaches and directors. In terms of motivation, Johnny and his teammates were more drawn to the fact that Toms River American almost made it to Williamsport two years ago than to anything that happened way back in the '90s. What happened in 2005 was recent history. It was still fresh.

But that didn't mean he didn't understand the past, and what it meant to the town. The main road through Toms River was called Little League World Champions Boulevard. "It's pretty hard to miss it," Johnny said.

And as he stood through another of his dad's killer practices in the summer heat, there was no question that Johnny knew what he wanted. It was the same thing he had been wanting since the summer before, ever since it began to seem possible to dream big. He respected the local history. But he wanted to make some.

"You guys gonna get us to Williamsport?" a coach of one of TRLL's younger teams asked him, waving as he passed Johnny on his way to a car in the parking lot.

"Yeah," Johnny replied. It was easier than giving the full answer. Johnny thought his team could do it, but he also knew that Toms River American was a marked bunch this summer. The other teams would be gunning for them, because they were defending champs. Johnny believed that he and his teammates were about to see every opponent's best game, because it was going to be directed at them. The days of sneaking up on people were over.

"Everybody thinks we're going to win," Johnny said, as much to himself as to the man walking by.

Johnny and Quintin had been teammates on the Red Sox this season, just as they were the year before. In fact, four of the All-Stars were Red Sox; Andrew and Mo were the others. Four came from the Yankees: Scotty, Ryan Fabricatore, Billy Sullivan and Austin Higgins. The other players were scattered about during the season: Vinny with the Angels, Chris Gulla with the White Sox, Pauly with the Rangers, and so on.

It was a familiar group, and all the boys knew that Johnny had little hesitation in giving his dad a hard time at practice. Johnny didn't mind pushing a few limits here and there; and he could live with the push-ups in exchange for the cheap thrill of talking back to the old man occasionally. But when it came to the game itself, Johnny didn't fool around. He was a hitter who delivered surprising power from his skinny, 90-pound frame, his swing the product of thousands and thousands of practice cuts that had developed his timing and given him exceptionally quick hands; and he already was far along in his baseball education, thanks in no small part to his dad. Johnny understood that power, for a hitter at this level, was to a great degree the result of bat speed—that is, hands that could quickly get a bat through the strike zone in time to make solid contact with a pitch. It was the result of timing, focus and concentration. Johnny had all three.

Johnny was also now beginning to understand how this related to being a good pitcher. The effective throwers were the guys who could disrupt a hitter's timing by constantly changing the speed and location of their pitches. Johnny had worked and worked on those facets. He threw scores of pitching sessions—"bull pens," as they're called by coaches—to develop his off-speed pitches. Following John's lead at Hit Dogs, Johnny worked on his conditioning and agility during the winter months, a time of year when other kids' attention turned to basketball or video games or just hanging out. As much as Johnny loved all of that, he had decided that he wanted to get his baseball game to a true All-Star level, which gave him more in common with his Toms River predecessors than he might have imagined. But the summer of 2006 was too uneven for him. He was better early in the season than he was down the stretch. He went stone cold as a hitter at the state tournament, and he wasn't as integral in all the success as he wanted to be. That just wasn't going to cut it in '07.

Johnny didn't want to be simply the coach's son. He wanted to earn his way onto the field and then stay there, and he had already decided that he wasn't going to be afraid to get dirty—or bloody, or sick, or whatever it took—once he arrived.

Without intending it, Johnny had grown into a perfect teammate for a guy like Scotty Ringel. Like Johnny, Scotty was a player who absorbed everything that his coaches and baseball instructors threw at him. And like Johnny, Scotty roiled on the inside, though you'd seldom guess it by seeing the tall, slender, placid-looking boy go jogging out to play his position.

"If you hear the kids hootin' and hollerin' in the dugout, you won't hear him," said his father, Scott. "He's more likely to be taking things in, processing them inside. But he likes for things to be just right, and he tries to make them perfect. He pushes himself very, very hard." And in that sense, Scotty had Johnny—and for that matter Quintin, the superb outfielder who was notoriously hard on himself—as company.

Both Johnny and Scotty would be 13 years old when they played their 2007 summer All-Star games, and the way they comported themselves on the field at times suggested the benefit of their ages. The two might get through six innings with barely a dozen words spoken between them, yet their teammates never had to wonder if they had come to play. In Scotty, John already had observed that personality last summer; Johnny's transformation into a more serious player was something that had taken longer to develop. It was all the more rewarding to John to watch his son gradually become a kid who was willing to want something more, who was willing to accept responsibility for his talent. This maturity, John felt, was the key to just about everything else in life.

Practice, of course, was a different matter. On this June day, as the players lowered themselves to the ground for the push-ups, John pulled Johnny aside. "You're the coach's son!" he said. "You can't be doing this stuff!" It was as much a plea as anything else.

But later, in the car on the drive home, as the air conditioner finally began to kick in and both father and son sipped a cool drink, the particulars of that day's disagreement faded into insignificance. Normal conversation resumed, even if John had to jump-start the talk. Over time, it simply became the ritual.

"All right, all right—I love you, John," the coach finally said to his son. "Now turn that radio off and let's talk about what happened."

Johnny acceded, as he always did. And that was the thing. John knew what he had in Johnny; their relationship was as strong as oak. The years of baseball, all that time on the field together, had forged in them a connection that felt impossible to break. The world could be falling apart, but John and Johnny could talk baseball, and in talking baseball they never had to worry about speaking the same language. "He's my son," John said one evening, "and he's a great kid, and he's becoming a very good baseball player."

Johnny also was part of a team that John genuinely liked. He had every reason to like it. With the exception of Drew and Clayton, two reserves who had essentially played their way into the All-Star conversation by having great regular seasons, this was the same roster that John had taken into the tournaments in 2006. John played it very straight in situations like this, submitting his request for players but assuming nothing until he got back the approved roster from the Little League board. John had been around long enough to see some of the nudge-and-wink that had undermined past boards, with members secretly agreeing to vote each other's children onto the All-Star squads in a quid pro quo manner. It never worked, not in the big picture—not if the goal was to win. John and his staff, by contrast, had put together their list of player requests a full year ago, before the '06 tourney, and it was simply the list of the best players they could think of within their league. The names had barely changed at all in a year, and the little change that did occur carried an emotional cost for John.

Although Drew and Clayton had clearly grown and improved to the point that they deserved a spot on the team, their inclusion could only come at the expense of one of the boys who had played on the All-Stars as an 11-year-old. John and his coaches, torn on what to do, first tried to mitigate the situation by adding a 13th spot to the roster (many Little League All-Star teams carry only 12 players because it makes for easier substitution patterns). But even at that, for Drew and Clayton to be added to the list, one name from the 2006 team had to be dropped. In the end, Adam Massoud, who had played outfield the year before for the All-Stars, received fewer votes from the board members than either Drew or Clayton, and thus was left off the list. "A gut-wrenching decision," John explained it. "It was basically between those three guys for two spots."

The board's difficult decision suggested a basic honesty in the league's wanting to deliver the best lineup it could, especially this year. But John and his staff had an easy sell. They had the right kids. Toms River American's summer of 2006 had made that much very clear.

◆ ◆ ◆

WHEN PAULY SCHIFILLITI THOUGHT BACK to his 11-year-old season with the All-Stars, the memory took on a dreamlike quality. It had just been so perfect. Everything fell into place. Pauly and his teammates started showing up at the fields expecting success. It was almost weird how confident the Toms River guys became in such a short time. And on top of everything, it was fun.

Pauly had already played for the All-Stars twice, at 9 and 10, and Coach John was definitely different from the coaches before him. The practices were harder, longer, and sweatier. Coach John asked for more production from his players than any of the coaches Pauly had played for in the past. He asked Pauly and the other guys to reach a new level, and he ran them repeatedly during the practices until partway through the summer, when the team began to understand this was the kind of effort that winning teams had to put in.

"I wouldn't trade you for any group of guys in the world," John said after a workout one day, and it became a line that he repeated often over the next year. But when Coach said it, it sounded like he really meant the words. Pauly had no trouble believing him, which made the boy want to perform well all the more.

All the kids began to feel that way, which in the end may have been John Puleo's great gift as a coach. With John leading the emotional charge, the players themselves began to see winning not as some sort of happy accident or the mere product of physical superiority, but the intended result of an actual plan that hard work had hammered into place.

John simply took up the position that it was possible to get over the hump based upon sheer effort and will—and that a little belief wasn't the worst place to begin looking for the secret to overcoming long odds. He thought that even little kids could fight their way past an intimidating opponent, if they could be encouraged to want to badly enough.

Looking at his 11-year-olds in 2006, John knew that he was building a solid foundation. He had hardly been handed a box of rocks; the kids had won their share. The Americans had made the finals of their very first tournament together, at age nine, with many of these same players. John realized that they had basically come up short on one decent play here or there, but there was no question about their ability to compete in games. In fact, they had shown plenty during that first tournament, a little-kid get-together in Barnegat, which had become something of a tradition for the first waves of All-Star teams in the area. It was there that Scott Ringel had the first glimmer that the team might accomplish something someday; the boys lost the second game they played, and fell into the loser's bracket, but then rallied to win six straight times and advance all the way to the finals. There was fire, even then.

As 10-year-olds, the team had gotten to the district final but lost—again—to Jackson. Three times that year, in three different settings, the Toms River Americans played Jackson, and three times they lost. Jackson was barely half as big as Toms River in terms of population, but it had experienced dramatic growth over the past decade, and new money was pushing in all over the area. The money fed the school system, the tax base and, of course, the baseball fever, which gripped most of the larger communities in and around Ocean County. The baseball facilities were top-notch. The interest was there. The success, and especially the thrill of stealing some of Toms River's thunder since the end of the 1990s, had stoked their baseball interest.

What the parents of the Toms River Americans came to love was how unimpressed John seemed by all of that, and how little he let it color his approach. John was a conventional man in many respects, and he had indeed taken his players back to a fundamental style of practice; but he was uncommon in other ways. He was not a screamer, for one thing, which for some of the new All-Stars was a fairly radical switch. John was positive to the point of Pollyanna, and he was aware of his own tendencies; as he put it, "I'm the guy who sees the rain outside and says, 'No! It's liquid sunshine!'"

John brooked no teammate-on-teammate dissent; one of his pet peeves was Little League kids ragging on other kids, and it was one of his few hard and fast dugout rules that there be no negativity. It was funny to Vinny, in the sense that Coach John ran such brutal practices but then became such a teddy bear at game time, constantly telling the guys how good they were and how well he thought they were about to do. During one of the early games in the summer of '06, with Toms River losing early, John simply called his players into a huddle and said, "It's about to change. It's about to go our way. This is going to be so great." Vinny and Pauly and a few of the guys looked at each other with arched eyebrows, but they loved playing for a man who had so much faith in them.

Right out of the gate in '06, John's practices began paying dividends for the Americans. They were sharp in the field; they were making plays, very sure-handed around the ball. Although they'd been given a fairly tough draw in the pool play, with games against difficult opponents like Holbrook and Brick American, they had Scotty and Chris Gulla pitching tremendously, and they fought their way into the District 18 tournament semifinals against Manchester. With the score tied 2–2, John reached out to Scotty to come in and pitch, and Scotty delivered one of his finest performances, throwing a shutout the rest of the way. Toms River eventually took a 4–2 victory that put them into the finals.

Jackson was the next opponent. The Jackson kids were the ones who handed the Americans their first defeat in the Barnegat tournament when they were 9. The Jackson team that beat Toms River in the district finals as 10-year-olds went on to capture the New Jersey state title. Heck, they'd even beaten Toms River back when the kids were 8 and they had to use pitching machines to make sure a strike got pitched before sundown. They just kept winning. It looked for all the world as though Jackson was close to becoming the kind of dynastic program that Toms River had once claimed for itself.

And then everything changed.

Going into the bottom of the sixth, the District 18 championship for 11-year-olds in the summer of 2006 was shaping up like all the other Jackson games that Toms River had played in recent years. Jackson, hitting and scoring consistently throughout the game, had a 7–4 lead. Its pitcher was a left-handed reliever whom the Americans were having trouble hitting. Toms River was down to its final three outs. Even at the Brick National Little League's complex, the neutral site chosen for the game, there was a feeling of déjà vu among the fans who crowded the bleachers and stood just beyond the outfield fences.

But in the dugout, John suddenly had had enough. As he watched Vinny pull on his batting helmet and await his turn, slightly grim-faced and nearly silent, John realized that it could be their mind-set that was defeating the Americans as much as anything. He had to act immediately, for whatever good it might do. Hastily he called the boys together.

"I don't care about Jackson," he declared. "I don't want to hear any more about Jackson. If we play Toms River Little League baseball, play for each other, treat our teammates like brothers, the sky's the limit. Just lace 'em up and let's go play. That's what we came here for, right? To play?"

"Yeah!" came the response.

"Then let's go do it!" John thundered.

His timing, as it turned out, was impeccable, for what John didn't know was that the game had changed even as he was delivering what might be his final speech of the summer. When the Toms River players turned away from their huddle and back to the field, John immediately saw that Jackson had changed pitchers. The lefty they couldn't hit was gone—the word was that his arm was sore—and in his place came a right-hander who, if his warm-up pitches were any indication, was having trouble throwing a strike.

"You know what to do," John said to his players. And so they did.

Patiently working the count, forcing the pitcher either

to stay outside the strike zone or offer them a hittable pitch, the Americans got themselves back in the game. With one out and a runner on first, Vinny fouled off a few pitches and finally drew a walk. The pitcher, clearly rattled, quickly walked Andrew right behind Vinny. Suddenly the bases were loaded—and the coach's son was coming to bat.

John tried to calculate what to say. If he came on too strong with his son, Johnny would sense the desperation in John's voice; yet John felt as if he had to say *something*.

"Hey, don't worry about it!" John finally barked. "You're not getting paid either way!"

Johnny stepped into the batter's box and flashed a brief smile as he did. Message received.

He wasn't up to bat for long. On the second pitch, Johnny saw a fastball he liked, and he timed his swing perfectly. He ripped a single to left, scoring the run that made it 7–5. Toms River had Quintin and Scotty coming up next. For the first time all day, Jackson looked beatable.

The first hurdle, though, was Quintin himself.

To John, Quintin's at-bat in the sixth inning was the culmination of a game-long experiment by the coach: trying to teach life lessons in real time. In the second inning, Q had hit a hard line drive that was caught for an out, and upon returning to the dugout he suddenly burst into tears, just furious and pouting, making a scene. John, coaching at third base, could see the other Toms River kids noticing Quintin's outburst. The boy stomped around the dugout, slamming his gear. In some respects, Quintin's actions were a classic 11-year-old response to the moment, but it was the worst example for a great player to set: Without meaning to,

Q was giving every other player permission to fall apart if things didn't go his way.

John took a deep breath, and made a decision. When the inning ended, he walked straight to the dugout and stopped Quintin before he could take the field.

"Quintin," he said, "sit down."

With that, John benched one of his three best players in the championship game against Jackson. But he had seen the opportunity to teach; and he couldn't have lived with himself if he let that pass. So it was Mo who jogged out to play center field in the third inning, in place of a boy whom most locals considered the best they'd ever seen at the position at his age. From John's perspective, it was the only move to make.

John loved Quintin unreservedly. He felt for the boy. Quintin was a tremendously sensitive kid, the son of divorced parents who had taken to spending time at the Puleos' home, and it was an arrangement that suited everyone. Diane provided for him as she did her own children, often setting an extra place for him at the dinner table without comment. The message was clear that Quintin was welcome anytime, for any reason, at any hour, and for as long as he wished to stay. Johnny and Q got along famously, but then almost everybody loved hanging out with Quintin: he was funny, quick with a quip—a good friend. Several of the All-Star parents openly marveled at Quintin's ability to keep a huge smile on his face day after day, and he did have a terrific, photogenic, baseball-card-ready smile. But what John knew, as both a coach and a father, was that Quintin processed almost everything from the inside out, and he had developed a tendency to put absurd amounts of pressure on himself to be perfect at baseball, a sport that he appeared to play for pure release as much as anything else.

"Baseball's a good outlet for him—he comes out, he smiles, he laughs. But he takes things to heart—and, man, he hates to lose," said Scott Ringel. "I'll give you a good example: Quintin played on the Red Sox, and when they were eleven they had a dominant team, right? We played them during the regular season and they beat us like twenty-five to zero. Then, in the playoffs, Scotty hit a home run to beat them in a game, and Quintin got so mad he wouldn't shake *my* hand afterward. I started laughing. I said, 'Come on, Quintin, you see the uniforms? I'm not in uniform!' But that's how much he was into it and how much it affected him when things didn't go well."

What it meant was that, at times like these, making a routine out could send Quintin into a real tailspin. It was happening right now, in the middle of the 11-year-old District 18 championship game, and John felt compelled to act.

"Just let it go," he said to Quintin, sitting down next to him in the dugout as the Toms River Americans went out to the field without him. "You've got to learn to let things go. You've got to have a short memory. Sooner or later, you've got to get over this hump, Quintin. It's not about you—it's about this team you're playing with."

With that, John got up and walked down the dugout, leaving Quintin to work through the words for himself. For three innings, Quintin sat while Mo played his spot in center field. And Q handled it. He calmed down, regained his composure and went to work cheering on his teammates, lost once again in the basic fun and intensity of the game.

By the top of the sixth inning, John had decided that Quintin was ready to get back out there and play defense, so he put Q back in for Mo in center field, as Little League rules allowed. And now, with the Americans back on offense, John's move paid its great benefit: Quintin stepped into the batter's box, and he looked calm, under control—a boy who was going to make good decisions, not panicky or emotional ones.

From the outside his subsequent walk was almost unremarkable. The Jackson pitcher was carefully avoiding giving up a big hit, and nothing really came close to the strike zone. Just like that, Q was on first base, and he had forced in another run to make the score 7–6. Mo was on his feet in the dugout, screaming to his teammates. Ryan was up against the fence as well, looking out onto the field. "We can do this!" Ryan bellowed, and he believed it. Scotty Ringel was coming up, after all. What could go wrong?

From Johnny's perspective, what followed was one of the best at-bats he'd ever seen—and it came when everybody in the park, Scotty most of all, knew how important it was. The parents and the kids were screaming in between every pitch; their voices rose to a crescendo as the ball made its way from the catcher back to the pitcher, then fell quiet again as the pitcher got ready to deliver his next throw. The Jackson pitcher was really bearing down; he knew that Scotty was the batter who could make or break the game. Down at the third-base coaching box, John figured, somehow, that his best player would find a way to help his team.

"One time," John said, mostly to himself. "Get it done this one time."

He needn't have worried. Scotty was cool in the moment. He fell behind one ball and two strikes, but he never exuded any panic; instead, he began tracking the pitches even more carefully. And Scotty could do something that most players his age could only dream of: foul off a pitch he didn't really like. He did so now. With throw after throw, the Jackson pitcher worked the outside corner, trying to get Scotty to chase something out of the strike zone, but Scotty just fouled each one away—four fouls in a row, then five. The tension ratcheted up with each pitch. Finally, on another outside fastball, Scotty didn't offer his bat; he let the pitch go by. From his spot beyond the center-field fence, Scott Ringel's heart dropped. He felt sure his son had just taken the third strike and would be called out. But the umpire didn't see it that way. He called the pitch a ball, making the count 2–2—and just that quickly, the momentum of the entire sequence had changed. It was as though Scotty had won the battle by surviving that pitch.

The Jackson pitcher was out of tricks. He had nothing left. He thought he had Scotty struck out, and it didn't happen; and the pitcher's concentration broke with that very call. Scotty watched the next two pitches sail well out of the strike zone, and he calmly trotted down to first base with his walk, knowing he had just forced Andrew home with the game-tying run. In the stands, the Toms River parents burst into cries of shocked enthusiasm. Scotty had just turned in perhaps the best batting appearance of his life that didn't actually yield a hit. The score was 7–7.

For Jackson, the motivation now was to survive the rally and get to extra innings, so the Jackson coach changed pitchers again. Johnny stood on third base, the potential winning run. He and his dad stood side by side, watching the new Jackson pitcher warm up. The kid, obviously nervous, was having a terrible time throwing a strike. A couple of times, he fired balls that missed the catcher entirely and made their way to the backstop, which in this ballpark was set almost 20 feet away from home plate.

"If he puts one back there like that," John said, "go score."

As soon as the game resumed, the new pitcher uncorked a wild one that flew past the catcher. Johnny never heard his dad say a word, because he didn't need to hear an instruction; he knew to take off the instant he saw the ball rolling free. As he raced down the line, he saw out of the corner of his eye that the Jackson catcher had tracked the ball and was gathering it up. The pitcher had raced in from the mound to take the throw and put a tag on Johnny—it was going to be that close. But even as he began to slide, Johnny knew he had won the game. The pitcher hadn't blocked the plate completely, and Johnny was able to brush his foot across home before the tag was applied. He felt as if the entire sequence was playing itself out in slow motion. Johnny lay there, safe at home, while the Toms River American kids sprinted toward him to begin the inevitable dog pile that signaled Little League victory. The baseball world, for these kids, had just spun off its axis. Jackson was finally on the wrong side of the score.

"We slayed the dragon," was how John put it, and for

the Americans that was really how it felt. Looking back, there wasn't a single member of the team who did not identify the Jackson game as the biggest he'd ever played. It validated everything that Coach John had been preaching about hard work and team spirit. The details were irrelevant; the fact was that Jackson gave back the game after having had such a perfect opportunity to close things out once again. John's players had just altered their own baseball trajectory, straight into a future they could begin imagining. And a team was formed.

THAT TEAM, IN THE SUMMER of '06, completely rewrote the chapter of possibilities for Toms River American, and it set the stage for what would happen in 2007. Scotty went on a tear as a pitcher in which he didn't allow a run for four or five games straight; newspaper articles wrote him up as a Greg Maddux–type player. Chris Gulla, so calm and controlled on the mound, delivered his finest performance in the section tournament in Robbinsville, matching a hard-throwing pitcher from Perth Amboy inning for inning, until Johnny Puleo, transformed by his success in the district title game, popped a home run for a 2–1 victory. It was Chris's shining hour, a game in which it was fair to say that his team absolutely would not have advanced without him. With Perth Amboy dispatched, the section was Toms River's to win, which the boys did by defeating Allentown, a glorious two-hit shutout pitched by Scotty. When Scotty then delivered another gem, a 9–0 victory over Washington Township in the first game of the state tournament on a field in Piscataway near the campus of Rutgers University, the state title loomed on the horizon, just a couple of days away.

As it developed, that game marked the last victory of the summer. The Americans quickly lost their next two contests, to Livingston and Franklin, and were put out of the state tournament. Both experience and fatigue came into play, especially at their age. Before the section championship game, on a particularly hot and humid day, Johnny had become so sick that he threw up. He spent that game as a spectator, alternating his time between the shade of the press box and the front seat of a car with the air conditioner running, Diane carefully looking after him. John, having removed him from the lineup, peered out constantly from the dugout, looking to see how Johnny was feeling; but per the rules, he could not allow Johnny to come sit with his teammates in the dugout unless Johnny was prepared to play. No one was willing to take such a chance with Johnny's health.

Though it could have been any number of things that made Johnny ill that day, and though what appeared to be heat stroke was gone the next day, his withdrawal was unsettling for everybody. Even amid all the good vibes, there was a sense that the Americans were pushing close to their limit. At the state tournament they finally hit it.

"We just didn't have it—we were all tired," said Chris Gulla. "It was a long drive up there [to the state tournament], and we were making the round-trip every day, and we kind of were worn out. We wanted to win, but you could tell some of the other teams were just more pumped up and ready to go.

"But, you know," he added, "we had already beaten

Jackson. That was it for us—that was our big game—because that's the team we could never beat. We beat Jackson. That's when we knew we were a good team. We finally did it."

It was a great summer, and it was a learning time. John had trusted his instincts about exactly how hard his team was going to have to work to be ready to win big, and he had been mostly right about that. Oh, he had small second guesses; if given the chance to do it over again, John would have encouraged the entire team to stay in Piscataway rather than make the hour-and-fifteen-minute drive each way from Toms River every day. The Americans had gone two months with either a practice or a game every day by the time their tournament run ended, and under any system of accounting, that was an awful lot of baseball for boys their age. As well as the players had performed, the schedule obviously had put a strain on kids and parents alike.

In talking to their kids and the coaches after the tournament, the parents chose their words carefully, though, in part because they were so thrilled by the success and in part because, to a person, they felt that John Puleo had been exactly the right coach at the right time. John had brought out the best in these boys; he had taught them how to be a team. One parent said, "If it were anyone else but John, I don't think there's any chance in the world that we do what we did in the summer of '06. Those kids were good kids, but the rest of the winning was all John. And I think we all knew that, and I think it's part of what made us tentative to criticize anything, really. Everybody was too busy having a great time."

But the physical toll was real. As much fun as the Amer-

icans had, the entire coaching staff realized—after the fact—
that they had ridden their horses just a mile too far, to the
point that they didn't have enough left in their reserves to
summon up a few more days of brilliant baseball at the state
tournament. Looking back, John and the others realized that
spotting the kids a rest day every week or so might have
worked wonders for their ability to continue bouncing back,
game after game.

"As a therapist, I work with sick people and injured
people, and I kind of understand the recovery period," said
Kelly Volk, Matt's mother and a devoted lifelong runner. "I
kept saying to the coaches, 'There's no recovery time here.'
These are children, not small adults, and they do need to re-
cover. They're growing, and their physiology is not like ours.
And I think I was kind of—I don't want to say resentful, but
I think I really did not understand at this age why we had to
be doing that, going every single day.

"I said to my husband, 'There's a difference between
quantity and quality.' I mean, fifty-something days: None of
us would work fifty days straight, without a day off. It bothered me—not for me, but for Mo. You can burn a kid out.
And I think that by the end of that summer, when we lost
at State, part of it was burnout. All those days and no breaks,
and we were just done."

Still, Kelly had kept her concerns mostly to herself. She
could see the bigger picture, which was that the kids kept
winning and kept coming home with smiles on their faces.
For Kelly, who grew up in Toms River and spent part of her
childhood at the Little League field with her three brothers,
John was the one who had helped the Americans learn how

to win as a team for the first time. Kelly had such an admiration for the coach, and the way that John communicated with the boys, that she tempered her worry over the constant workouts and the physical and mental toll they could take. John might work them into the ground, but he'd be the first person to pick them up again—and as a parent, Kelly truly appreciated the fact that John could prompt the boys to do things the way he wanted them done without resorting to screaming. And though she knew that the 1998 team winning the World Series had changed the perspective on Little League in Toms River in ways that weren't always healthy, she was right there with every other parent of the Americans, reveling in the victories, allowing herself to daydream about her son and his teammates going to Williamsport. It wasn't the world, no; Kelly and Jerry were, above all, level-headed parents. But it wasn't for nothing, either. The World Series was a breathtaking goal. It was worth pursuing.

And if they could attain that goal, if Toms River American could get on a roll and follow it to Williamsport in 2007, then no one would talk about the rigors of the practices, except in glowing terms. In truth, John always suspected that most of the teams around the Jersey Shore had worked out about as hard as his did—most of the serious ones, anyway. He didn't kid himself that the coaches, players and parents from Jackson or Brick had suddenly decided to take it easy and cruise through the district. All of the big teams ramped it up. John was simply the first coach to bring that work ethic to this collection of young guys.

In the weeks after the '06 run ended, though, John carried around the nagging thought that perhaps he pushed his players one peg too far. Maybe he went over the top. He probably could have given the boys a day off here and there without losing the momentum they'd built up over the months. All in all, it sounded reasonable. It was a safe bet.

But something deep inside John would not allow for that, for even taking the chance. It was a fact that John acknowledged openly: he feared not having done enough to win, and he knew he couldn't live with himself if he felt he could have done more. There was within him a wellspring of doubt—John would describe it as negativity—that was the residue of a time when he lived as a different person, someone whom John vowed the Toms River American kids would never meet.

Before any of his kids were born, before he and Diane were even married, 15 years ago, John was a gambler. His habit was pathological. Running multiple bets on a single day was like breathing; it was what John did. He was a fully functional addict; he held down his job—built Beta Graphics into a business during that time, in fact—and managed to meet and court Diane. He had a life. But he also had a life within his life, and his first love, his deep connection, was to gambling.

For John, living a gambler's life meant almost constantly worrying about this bet or that one, making a point spread, agonizing over the unforeseen injury that could cause a game to suddenly lurch in the direction of a money-loser. His everyday existence revolved around factors that, strictly speaking, were beyond his control. He had ceded that control to the bet itself. Over time, it ate him up.

Ultimately, John was rescued by the woman who would become his wife, on a trip to a bed-and-breakfast that she had arranged for his birthday in October 1992. The Toronto Blue Jays were playing the Philadelphia Phillies in the World Series. The college football season was in full swing. The NFL had already cranked up the machinery. The bed-and-breakfast was nothing but a backdrop.

"I was a stone-cold loser," John said. "The Series, college football, pro football—I must have had fifty bets. Fifty different games that day, and I was on the verge of a nervous breakdown. Diane slapped me in the face about ten times and she said, 'Go to Gamblers Anonymous or we'll never get married.' And I owe her. I owe her for saving my life."

Fifteen years later, in the summer of '07, John Puleo had never laid down another bet. He was a regular at GA meetings, going to at least one a week. Fending off the itch to gamble had simply become another part of his life; it was something he did all the time. He carried it around with him, along with the tools to beat it, and it shaped his view of the world. It shaped his view of how to coach a child's game like Little League.

None of which was to suggest that John didn't care about winning or losing. Quite the opposite: His approach to Little League was geared toward getting win after win after win. His only hesitation in discussing his past, in fact, was the concern that people might hear his story and mistakenly walk away thinking that he was congratulating himself for reducing the meaning of victory.

"He wouldn't want anyone to think that his thought process was, 'Oh, we lost, but it's okay because I know what really grounds me,'" said Diane. "It would be wrong to make it sound like the Little League games weren't important, because they were very important to him."

Of that there was little question, especially when Williamsport swung fully into view. But John didn't coach only for those wins. The games, to him, were supposed to be a good time—and the practices, too. A hard time? Sure. But a good time.

"With baseball, I set as my goal simply to be with John and Matt. It's the reason I also coach Sophia in basketball," John said. "And deep down, I pray that they stay away from pathological addictions. My addiction is currently arrested— but I will always need Gamblers Anonymous."

John's children, he said, never saw him in gambling mode. "My wife has, but my kids have never seen the crazed animal that I used to be before I got married," he said. "And, God bless them, they shouldn't have to see it. It's not a normal way of living, you know. *This* is normal. And I'm very grateful, very grateful. People always joke with me, like, 'You're going down to the Little League field again? You're gonna get divorced!' But the reason why I do it is that I don't want to see them make the same mistakes I did."

It was a point of view that infused almost every decision John made, including the way he dealt with his Toms River American All-Stars. He wanted them responsible, but happy. He wanted them loose, but determined. He wanted them to be able to play like ferocious beasts for two hours, and then laugh and smile as they walked off the field together. John wanted it all.

◆ ◆ ◆

A T T H E E N D O F T H E summer of 2006, the disap-
pointment at being eliminated from the 11-year-old state
tourney wore off quickly, for two reasons: First, too many
good things had happened for anyone to be truly unhappy
about losing a couple of games; second, it was but a preview
of 2007. The 2006 All-Star experience gave the team the
confidence that it could win big, and it left the boys with
goals still to be achieved. They suddenly couldn't wait for
next summer. The sooner they got back in play, the sooner
they could resume the fun.

CHAPTER 4

A DULL ACHE IN THE ARM

CHRIS GULLA WAS ACHING. HE wasn't hurting the way kids sometimes say they're hurting; he didn't have a stomach pain or tired legs, or a heat cramp, or anything temporary like that. He wasn't asking out of practice drills. He didn't need to: He couldn't do the drills at all. Chris could barely lift his pitching arm, because, frankly, it had been all but blown out by a season filled with injury, stress and some hideous bad luck.

The Americans had less than a week remaining before their first game in the 2007 District 18 tournament. The boys were to play Berkeley on June 27, and even if Berkeley didn't line up as the most imposing team in the bracket, the point was that, from then on, the baseball games came in bunches, and you had to be ready to respond physically. The coaches hadn't even been allowed to contact the players and schedule a first workout before June 15, which meant the clock had been ticking from the instant they got together. It was a 12-day window for them to prepare for the run to

Williamsport that they had been imagining ever since the state tournament the year before.

Now the 12 practice days had dwindled to six, and as John Puleo's eyes followed Chris around the field at Mapletree during the evening workout, he could see clearly that Chris was in no position to do anything that related to throwing a baseball. Since John had hoped to use Chris as one of his top two pitchers, this was a development to consider.

The injury had been coming for a while—months, actually. Chris didn't even make it out of the exhibition portion of the Little League regular-season schedule in one piece. He was behind the plate, doing the catching for his team, the White Sox, in an early spring game when the batter fouled off a pitch. Catchers are taught to put their "free hand" behind their backs when receiving a pitch, thus catching the ball with only the hand that is already protected by the mitt. In this case, as the foul ball angled back toward him, Chris couldn't help himself. He reached out reflexively to stop it with his right hand—his pitching hand. His unprotected, uncovered pitching hand.

It was a human sort of impulse, to block the ball from getting away from him, and even though it was a foul it was fairly common. Pitchers accidentally did so all the time, suddenly thrusting a bare hand forward to stop a ball about to rifle past them on the ground or on a line drive. Instinct. In Little League, coaches spend an awful lot of time programming out certain impulses, like this one. And what happened to Chris next is exactly the reason why: The foul ball ricocheted off his right thumb. Instantly, he knew it was bad.

But being a kid, Chris figured it was just a really sore

bruise. He shook his hand a few times, trying to get the sting out. He said very little to anyone about it. After all, he had been able to wiggle the thing right away. If the thumb was broken, he wouldn't be able to move it, would he? He thought he remembered hearing that somewhere. When his parents asked, Chris told them it was sore, but that he could flex it. He went home and put some ice on the area where the ball struck, and when practice rolled around the next time, he took the field like he always did. He wasn't going to quit playing baseball because he took a hard shot off his thumb. For that matter, Chris's response was the rough equivalent of the old baseball admonition, "Rub some dirt on it." He'd just play until the hurt finally went away, and he would avoid throwing many pitches while it got better. That seemed like a good plan.

And, of course, it didn't work. Two weeks later, attempting to pitch in a game against the Yankees, Chris found himself facing his All-Star teammate, Scotty Ringel. His first pitch sailed wildly off course and hit Scotty—"Right on the butt," Chris's mom, Donna, remembered with a slight smile—and that was all Donna needed to see to confirm what she had begun to suspect: Chris wasn't right. She took him to a doctor, and the news was bleak: a broken thumb that needed to be cast immediately in order to begin healing, especially since so much time had elapsed between the injury and the diagnosis. Now Chris was going to have the cast on for a month. There was no telling yet whether he had done any more damage by playing for those two weeks.

The season was about to become a scramble for Chris—and a faraway worry for Coach John. Since Chris was not a member of his Red Sox team, John had very little contact with him during the Little League season, but he sure knew what was going on. He also knew the All-Star rules, which stated clearly that no player could be eligible for the summer tournaments if he did not suit up for at least half of his team's games during the regular season. The thumb's healing process was progressing, but the baseball opportunity was so fleeting, and so important. "We were very concerned about All-Stars," Donna said.

To Chris, as Donna and her husband, Dennis, knew, the All-Stars were everything. Not only did making the team represent the pinnacle of the year for a player, but Chris, in particular, was coming off that incredible summer of 2006, when he was a lights-out pitcher and hit a couple of home runs, too. John went so far as to call Chris "dominant," which was not a term that Chris had heard applied to his game before. It brought a smile to his face and gave him a new perspective on how good he might actually become. But, according to the other coaches, it was not hyperbole: When Chris was on his game, especially as a pitcher, he was tough to beat.

He had three pitches: a fastball, a regular changeup and this strange, erratic-moving knuckle curve, the pitch that he and a friend had invented years ago while goofing around playing catch in the neighborhood. It was a Toms River tradition to develop such a pitch out of playing ball in the yard, and Chris knew he wasn't the first to come up with an unusual grip or way of throwing the ball. He'd heard stories of other kids who had tried their own pitches in games. But his knuckle curve, in which he literally placed a knuckle on top of the baseball, wasn't a pitch very many kids could throw, and when it worked it really messed up the hitters. The ball came in slow, without the natural rotation that a fastball had, and it appeared to move around on its way to the plate. It was a pitch that sometimes caused Chris to smile through his braces, standing there on the mound, when he threw it right.

He'd used that pitch repeatedly in 2006, and it succeeded far more often than it failed. Of course, you also needed a viselike thumb grip on the side of the baseball to make that pitch work—or any other pitch, for that matter. The weeks went by, and both Chris and his folks came to the realization that it would be lucky if he just got his throwing rhythm back in time for the All-Stars—and that assumed that he could appear in enough games with the White Sox to qualify at all.

Because of Chris's thumb, even as he coached his Red Sox through the regular season, John was changing his likely All-Star pitchers. If Chris wasn't on the team, then people like Johnny and Andrew Hourigan, whom John had hoped to use in supporting roles on the mound, would have to step up. *Somebody* had to be the second stud alongside Scotty. That's how you won in All-Star competition. It was how Mike Gaynor's teams punched their way through to the holy land in all three of those years in the '90s; Gaynor had two great pitchers on each of those teams whom he could alternate in the big games, and then he had a group of decent throwers who could come in and get him an inning or two, or even just a couple of outs. You could get through it if you had two horses on the mound. Based on his performance last summer, Chris was supposed to be one of those two.

After a month, Chris returned to the field, and as it turned out, the early-spring weather actually worked to the advantage of the Gulla family and the All-Stars. Because rain had forced the postponement of so many early-season games, their schedule was nowhere near half over by the time Chris was able to rejoin the team. He would be able to satisfy the eligibility requirement. The question was whether he could really play.

And play he could—until he felt a new pain, in a different place.

The second injury of Chris Gulla's season was almost stranger than the first. He had returned; he was back in action; he could pitch again. He was beginning to find his location and velocity on the mound again, and the White Sox, who were gunning for a league title, couldn't welcome him back fast enough. Even with Chris at less than 100 percent, they certainly didn't have anyone better. In fact, the White Sox pitched Chris every chance they got, including heavy rotation in the Little League playoffs.

His heavy workload was a normal part of the Little League experience, and it owed substantially to the fact that the Majors division of the league is unlike any other. From the tee-ball years on through, all of the minor-league levels of the organization are primarily teaching situations, but Majors is an abrupt departure. Within the overall structure of a Little League charter, the local leagues have the ability to allow anyone from age 9 to 12 to play at the Majors level, but the difference between, say, a fourth-grade boy and a seventh-grade adolescent can be staggering—and nowhere is that difference more obvious than when a young hitter faces a much older pitcher. Their physical mismatch alone ensures that the younger player, even if he's a great athlete, will fail far more often than he succeeds. It's just about impossible for a little kid to hit a screaming fastball from a 12-year-old who may be twice his size.

Thus, most coaches find themselves leaning heavily on their big guys to pitch as often as they can take the ball. Chris was not alone in being used fairly constantly. Another of John's favored pitchers, Pauly, hit the All-Star team with something less than his best stuff, his tired throwing arm the result of having been used so much by his team, the Rangers, during the regular season.

"We were all watching, really watching, like, 'Oh, my god, they're pitching Pauly again,'" said his mother, Lisa. But from Pauly's perspective, the playing time he received was normal. "They overused me," he said, "but they didn't force me to. I wanted to pitch." And his dad, Anthony, went out of his way to deflect blame from any of the regular-season coaches. Anthony's view was simply that the Rangers looked up to Pauly and wanted him to pitch anytime he felt that he could, and that it was Pauly's choice, in the end, whether to take the ball or not. As long as the team wasn't violating any league restrictions on pitching, all was fair.

"A lot of kids completely obliterated their arms during the regular season," said John's assistant Jerry Volk. "You want to get mad at the other coaches, but they're out there with ten-year-olds trying to play Majors. And this is their World Series. This is their All-Stars. Of course they're going to go with the older guys."

So when Chris came back to the regular season, he

pitched, and then he pitched some more. When the White Sox advanced all the way to the league finals in early June, Chris's team squared off against John's Red Sox. With the pressure on, Chris pitched a remarkable game for the win and the league championship. The White Sox went on to play in the city championship and in the Tournament of Champions, a collection of the best regular-season teams from around the area.

But away from the field, Chris was in trouble. Though he hadn't been telling anybody, he was feeling pain in his pitching arm. It sometimes hurt just to play catch with his buddies in the neighborhood, especially on days after he had pitched a Little League game. And Chris was an all-sport kind of a kid. In a perfect world, he'd go from football in the fall to basketball in the winter, then baseball again in the spring. Over this past winter, he had junked that schedule after talking it over with his folks. Coach John had kept the Bengals team playing through the fall, and then had the Hit Dogs workouts over the winter. Chris gave up football for the season, and it seemed like a fair thing to do; after all, the All-Stars were going for the Little League World Series. But now, here in June, struggling with a bad arm that sometimes ached even when he went outside just to ride his skateboard, Chris realized that the heavy rotation of baseball, baseball and more baseball had left a mark.

"It was probably just too much for him, too much throwing," John Puleo said. "Who knows? There's always the debate between too much throwing and not enough throwing. You sometimes hear that the kids now are underused so much that they never do build up their arms. But with Chris, I think it was probably the other way."

The arm said so. Just after the Red Sox game in the league championship, Chris found that his right forearm felt even tighter than usual. Again, he assumed the pain might go away; instead, it got worse. Within a week, he could not throw a baseball at all. Donna and Dennis suspected tendonitis, for which the only real prescription was rest, and after his mom took him to a chiropractor who came to the same conclusion, Chris was given a brace and was told to take it easy. The thing was, All-Stars were about to begin.

At selection time in early June, John and the coaches didn't hesitate to put Chris on the roster. They all felt that Chris had earned his spot on the team by virtue of his terrific work the year before. Moreover, sore arms often came with the territory, and they usually went away.

Now, though, the tournament was barely a week off, and Chris still wasn't showing any sign of coming around. The boy was willing, but John didn't want to risk further injuring Chris's arm; he went out of his way to see that Chris laid low. During the ground ball drills, Chris was instructed to field the ball and then hand it to a teammate, who would complete the throw. John wouldn't even let Chris do push-ups. The only thing Chris was allowed to do in full was swing the bat, because he said the motion caused him no pain.

The question of what to do when the games rolled around was something else again. Based on their performances in 2006, Scotty and Chris were the top two pitchers, with Pauly, Johnny and Andrew all likely to throw significant innings. But John had to adjust for the injury factor with Chris. He had been tracking Chris's recovery from the broken thumb, but now Chris was fighting a different battle:

He didn't appear eager to start pitching again when All-Stars began. "The injuries made Chris tentative," Jerry Volk observed. "We didn't see the fire in his eyes. I think he was a little worried that something else would go wrong—or that he wouldn't be good enough."

In truth, though, Chris's experience mirrored a national trend: an alarming uptick in the reported number of cases of arm and elbow problems for players of high school age and younger. In particular, there had been a dramatic increase in the number of young players requiring surgeries to repair pitching-related injuries. What grabbed national attention were the comments of reconstructive specialists like Dr. James Andrews, the Alabama-based surgeon to the sports stars. Andrews noted that his own practice was performing higher and higher numbers of "Tommy John" procedures (the reconstruction of a damaged elbow ligament with a tendon taken from somewhere else in the body) in boys who were of high school age or younger. Andrews and research partner Dr. Glenn Fleisig stood at the forefront of a movement to restrict the number of pitches that younger players could be allowed to throw in any given week, arguing that their studies and case histories had shown the single highest risk factor for arm and elbow problems in young baseball players was their tendency to pitch well past the point of fatigue.

The numbers were sobering across the board. Andrews and Fleisig's research found that, among athletes age 14 to 20, the pitchers who routinely threw more than 80 pitches in a game were four times as likely to require surgery as those who threw less than that. Those who said they pitched in eight or more months out of a calendar year were five times more likely to need a surgical procedure. And those who agreed that they normally pitched past the point of fatigue were 36 times more likely to require surgery than those who either were pulled or asked out of a game when they were spent. The implication, of course, was obvious: Young players were pitching deep into games because they felt their teams were counting on them, and those players' coaches, even well intentioned, were harming the kids by leaving them on the mound.

Andrews and Fleisig argued that a pitch count was one of the most effective ways to combat the trend toward overuse, and it was the pitch-count rule that Little League ultimately embraced—a radical departure from its longstanding policy of simply allowing each pitcher six innings of work per week. The new system was controversial and fairly complicated. It laid out not a maximum number of pitches allowed per week, but rather a mandatory rest period in between pitching performances that was tied to the number of pitches thrown on any given day. In the Majors division, if a pitcher threw more than 20 pitches in a game, he had to rest one calendar day. More than 40 pitches meant two calendar days of rest, and more than 60 required three days of rest before he could pitch again. The maximum number of pitches that could be thrown in any single game was 85 per pitcher.

That Little League moved so aggressively on behalf of its young pitchers was both salutary and, in terms of reaction, a bit of a reach. Anecdotally, at least, it appeared that Little League was trying to solve a problem it hadn't had much to do with creating. The rise of ancillary "travel" or "competi-

tive" leagues, and their booming popularity throughout the
United States, was closer to being a cause of elbow injuries than was Little League's schedule, which hadn't changed
over the years. Under Little League, baseball was basically a
spring and summer sport. But the leagues and associations,
put together by alphabet-soup organizations like the Amateur Athletic Union, United States Specialty Sports Associa-
tion and others, functioned as all-weather, all-comers hosts.
Anyone who could pony up the fee of nearly $500 per team
could enter a weekend tournament, provided the birth cer-
tificates of the players checked out. Teams were permitted
to play in multiple age groups, thus allowing a roster full of
10-year-olds to play in an 11-Under tourney one weekend,
a 12-Under bracket the next weekend, a 10-Under playoff
the following week. The teams traveled all over their area,
around their region, even across the country and back, depending mostly upon what their parents and coaches decided they wanted to do—and pay.

Excess was everywhere, particularly where pockets were
deep. Stories abounded of high-end, heavily funded teams
from Georgia or Texas having players flown in to tournaments—just to pitch in a single game. Some teams, despite
fielding rosters full of kids who weren't yet approaching
puberty, had locked onto corporate sponsors like Rawlings,
allowing them to travel several states away for a single weekend of baseball.

But most significant was the fact that the leagues essentially operated year-round, especially in places like Florida
and California, where the weather was cooperative most of
the time and to which teams from other states wanted to

travel and play. In a time in which even youth sports had fallen victim to the insidious disease of specialization, it was increasingly common to see an 11- or 12-year-old play base-ball 10 months out of the year. Partly as a result, kids were being wildly overused on the pitching mound, sometimes shuttling back and forth between Little League and travel ball in the same week or even the same weekend. Beyond that, many young players were being pulled out of Little League altogether, the better for their parents to steer them toward what they considered to be the more serious, high-level competition being offered by the travel leagues, with the accompanying physical intensity of playing four or five games in a two-day span. Often the parents moved aggres-sively but stupidly, failing to take into consideration the pos-sibility of injury or burnout that could follow the slotting of their children on a single-sport track. The leagues played to the parents' fears that their sons and daughters were some-how falling behind if they did not play a particular sport year-round.

It was all a bit disorienting to the average volunteer who came out of the stands to coach his or her son's Little League team. Still, Little League felt compelled to address the reality that many of its youths risked serious, long-term injury if they weren't forcibly restrained from throwing so many pitches.

From his vantage point as the coach of three World Series entries, Mike Gaynor found himself loudly doubt-ing the entire enterprise. Gaynor's experience had led him to the firm conclusion that the problem, at least for Little League, had to do with kids pitching too little, not too much. They needed to build up their pitching arms, Gaynor thought, rather than be constantly coddled and thus prevented from gaining the strength to throw a game's worth of pitches.

"The whole pitch-count thing is bull," Gaynor said, "because it has nothing to do with Little League. Little League got the rap for all this crap because all these kids are getting themselves hurt, but they're getting hurt because they're playing twelve months out of the year. Little League for us was usually one game a week, six innings. You can't get hurt throwing one game a week for six innings."

Under the new rules, Gaynor noted, players could throw as many as 85 pitches in a game, then take only the required three days' rest before pitching again. "So you can throw eighty pitches on Monday and then come back Friday and throw eighty more pitches. Under the old rules, you could only throw six innings for the week, period. If you threw the six on Monday, you weren't coming back until the following week. But it was all politics, and they felt they had to do something because Dr. Andrews was saying, 'I'm cutting more kids than I ever cut in my life.' Yeah, but why blame that on Little League? Because they're the big dogs, is why."

Actually, Dr. Andrews's suggestions were tied more to the idea of preventing a player from pitching well past his fatigue point in any one game; but even that idea would have been lost on Gaynor's teams from the '90s. Those teams, Gaynor said, trained to pitch. Their pitchers threw live batting practice, facing their own teammates, every day. The work load wasn't overwhelming, often limited to 30 or so pitches, but it was constant. As Gaynor put it, "They threw every single day. I moved the strike zone in and out, inside corner, outside corner. I called pitches and had the kids throwing to spots. By the time we got to games, they could hit that strike zone with their eyes closed." Beyond that, Gaynor often had more than one of his pitchers throw the batting practice to his team in the hours before a game. He sometimes used those pre-pregame practices, with his pitchers facing their own Toms River East hitters, to help him decide whom to start in that day's contest. He lost no one to a sore arm.

That was then. In 2007, the new pitch-count rules were in place, and Chris Gulla was a huge question mark. John was going to have to figure out what to do. He scanned the roster, and he saw what he saw. Johnny could certainly pitch. Pauly had the knuckle changeup and could be counted on for a few innings when needed. Andrew Hourigan was pretty much good at whatever he did, and could get on the mound if needed. Billy Sullivan wasn't a front-liner, but he could reliably throw a strike, and, as perhaps the most relaxed player on the field, he wasn't afraid to take the ball. Not much was going to rattle or bother him.

All together, the pitching staff wasn't overwhelming. In fact, absent Chris, it wasn't terribly impressive. It appeared that the Americans of 2007 were going to need to field their positions very well, and perhaps produce a little more offense than they had the summer before, if they were going to persevere long enough for Chris to really return and make a difference as a pitcher. John already was worried that Scotty might not be as dominant as he had been a year ago. Scotty was now in seventh grade, and as such he was playing on his intermediate school team in addition to Little League. The seventh-grade team used a larger field than Little League, with the pitching mounds set farther away from home plate. Scotty was constantly shifting back and forth between the different distances, and each time he came back to Little League, throwing from only 46 feet away rather than 60, it always took him a while to get his pitching motion adjusted.

Watching Chris stand idle and Scotty struggle with the distances, John understood that the situation had changed from the summer before. In retrospect, that year had been remarkable not just for the quality of baseball but for the absence of any roster-changing injury. Even Johnny's heat sickness had affected only one game. This time around, the All-Stars hadn't even reached their first game, and their coach already found himself wondering what the roster might look like if it were without one of its primary players.

CHRIS'S INJURY PUT A DISQUIETING spin on the practice atmosphere, in part simply because it made a good kid visibly unhappy. Chris was a pleaser at heart; a compliment from Coach John was enough to make him happy for the rest of the day. And Chris had always been good; he had made every All-Star team since he was nine. Now he stood on the practice field, the days quickly counting down to the first district game, and he struggled to feel a part of the team. He stopped joining in the practice chatter, sometimes falling completely silent, and there wasn't really anything anybody could say. You could only ask him, "How's it feeling?" so many times.

But Chris's injury wasn't the only difference from the year before. A lot had changed since 2006. Despite the boys' easy chemistry and John's habit of cranking up music from his truck's stereo during practice to keep the mood upbeat, it became apparent that the pressure to win was creeping in. The Toms River Americans had never before played the role of front-runner—that job had been Jackson's ever since the nine-year-old tournament in Barnegat. Their status came with a few surprises. It had begun during the regular season, as parents told stories of seeing coaches from other Little Leagues sometimes stopping by the Mapletree complex, watching the games and scouting the talent they'd likely be matched against in All-Stars. "There were always a lot of people watching our games. It was weird," Johnny Puleo said.

Jackson wasn't the defending district champ; Toms River American was. And now that the Americans had done it once, there were no excuses for not winning again.

"I had the Red Sox all season, and they had a great year, but as soon as the season was over it was time to get pumped up," John said. "I knew that this was an opportunity that these kids had. They were talented enough to do it. All we'd ever heard was about Jackson, but now we had beaten Jackson, too. Snatched that game from the depths of a loss is what we did. So now it was Toms River's time to be the favorite again, after all those years. We saw what our own league had done in 2005, so we had a road map. And it started with having goals."

One of the small gifts of the summer of '06 was that everything was a first, and in some ways it was an advantage to lack any clear sense of the way the All-Star season "ought" to go. In that sense, their experience had paralleled Mike Gaynor's first World Series team, the one from 1995. It mirrored the Toms River East All-Stars in most of the good ways, and especially in that sense of not exactly knowing what came next. And it proved a remarkably useful bit of ignorance.

"I always use this analogy about '95: You know how things are always bigger and better on the other side, like you feel you're doing well on the mountain, and you cross it, and the next mountain ahead of you is just bigger and better? Well, it seemed like every tournament, we thought we'd see bigger and better competition," Gaynor said. "And every time we'd come home with a victory, we were thinking, 'How's this happening? Why is this happening to us?' It was just—we were just Toms River, you know? We'd never done anything. There were no expectations on us. Everything we did was a breakthrough. I mean, we weren't even sure that the way we were preparing for the games was the right way to go. It wasn't until the second time around, in '98, that I really felt like I knew how to get my team ready to play. That first time, it opened the doors for everybody. I kept pinching myself, like, 'When are we going to get our asses kicked?' But it never happened, and I never felt that way after that, never again when it came to one of our teams. And I think that feeling rolled through the town after that, that it's not someone else's dream. It's not always some kid from Texas or North Carolina. Sometimes it's a kid from Toms River."

In the case of the Americans, though, their breakthrough season had come not in their World Series–eligible year, but the year before. A full year had passed, and it had been a year of open conversation—not just among the boys, but around them as well.

"All the coaches in Little League, they were like, 'You gonna get that Williamsport trophy this year?'" Pauly said. "They were all waiting for us to do it—wanting it. And everyone else, from outside our league, they wanted to take us down. It was like you had a target on your back. To the other teams, it didn't matter how it turned out: If they beat us, it was amazing; if they lost, they lost to the team that won third place in the state. They could play loose, because if they lost, so what? That was definitely different."

John sensed the difference, too. He had heard plenty of the chatter over the winter. Really, John had been hearing the talk all along, going back to the fall of 2006, when he organized the Bengals traveling team as a way to keep his All-Stars playing together for as long as possible. Now he had six days to the first All-Star game, and no firm idea about what Chris Gulla, his erstwhile hero, was going to be able to give him. It was time to start making something up.

CHAPTER 5

DEEP END OF THE POOL

WHAT SCOTTY RINGEL WAS TRYING to deliver, in a way, was a sense of normalcy. He wanted to turn in a performance that reminded people of the year before. It didn't have to be perfect, just familiar.

John Puleo obviously felt the same way, or he wouldn't have sent Scotty out to the mound to start the first game of the 2007 District 18 tournament on June 27. After all, the opponent was Berkeley, not traditionally a huge threat. John could have been forgiven for wanting to hold Scotty back if he could, because the road was going to get dramatically more difficult from here. But in the complicated math of the playoff system, he didn't feel he had the luxury.

For Toms River American, the tournament's draw into its two pools of competing teams had proved to be about as bad as possible. In fact, it was so difficult that it left a contingent of parents and coaches wondering about the selection process—and noting, albeit in quiet tones, that the district administrator who made the assignments had been from one of the competing Little League programs. From their admittedly biased viewpoint, it sure looked like somebody was trying to mess with the Americans.

Because District 18 was so large, the tournament annually was divided into two sides. Each side, Pool A and Pool B, comprised seven teams. After each team played four games, the pools were reduced to the four top teams in A and B, and those eight teams would then proceed to a single-elimination playoff from which a district champion would quickly emerge. Depending on the strength of the pools, a team could go just 2–2 in the early games and still advance to the elimination round—but it wasn't advised. Going 3–1 or 4–0 was the only safe route to the playoffs. John intended to get his team there safely.

But there was no easy way around the bracket. Regardless of which pool a team was placed in, it was going to face difficult opponents, and once the eight teams advanced to the quarterfinals, there wouldn't be a weak sister in the bunch. But the timing and quality of each opponent was critical all the same. An easy early-round schedule, for example, could give a team the flexibility to use some of its second-tier pitchers in those games and save the A-list throwers for the showdowns. That was the dream scenario.

In that respect, Puleo's team had come up woefully short. The Americans figured to win their game against Berkeley, but after that the schedule grew dramatically more complicated. Toms River's second game was against Brick American, a team rumored to have a pitcher capable of throwing 75 miles per hour from the 46-foot distance. In terms of a batter's response time, such velocity would be the rough equivalent of a Major League Baseball pitcher delivering a 97-mph fastball. In order to make contact, a batter would almost have to start swinging the instant the pitch was released, which it turn suggested that he was either going to have to guess correctly, or find some other way to prepare for such blazing speed. Either way, Brick American was trouble.

But that was only the start. When the schedules were posted, John was astonished to see that his team had been placed in the same pool, Pool A, as its own league rival, Toms River National. Among the traditional powers in District 18, this was the only such assignment on the board: the two Toms River East teams had been split into separate pools; Jackson and Holbrook, the neighboring Little Leagues that had been coming on strong for the last several years, were separated into the A and B draws; and Brick National and Brick American would not cross paths until at least the sudden-death quarterfinal bracket.

But not Puleo's team. In fact, its final game of the pool-play round was to be a contest against Toms River National, held at the Mapletree complex on a Friday night in July. That game was sure to be an emotional and draining tussle in front of a packed house; it might very well determine the Americans' seeding for the elimination round; and it was scheduled to go off barely a day and a half before the Sunday afternoon quarterfinals, when the rubric became win or go home. All in all, lousy news—a great game for the fans and parents, but lousy news just the same.

John, Paul, Jerry and Scott discussed the schedule almost daily during the two weeks of practice. The final practice days before the Berkeley game confirmed that Chris wasn't ready yet, but he was making some progress with his sore arm, and John felt that he might be able to play Chris by Game 2 against Brick American. But John felt that he couldn't risk going into the Brick game with a 0–1 record and risk falling to 0–2 if Chris didn't have it. His decision was to send Scotty out there in the first game to nail down a victory.

The Americans' other problem had to do with its final two pool-play contests. Their third game was scheduled against Holbrook, and the word around the district was that Holbrook's kids had grown so much that they were almost unrecognizable from the year before. They were big and strong, capable of hitting baseballs to places where they couldn't be found. And the Americans were due to face them at the Holbrook Little League field, which was notorious for its short fences and its pop flies that, off the bats of strong 12-year-olds, suddenly sneaked over those fences for cheapie home runs.

Worse for John, the Holbrook game was scheduled for Thursday evening, with the Toms River National game looming the following night. John knew enough about his cross-league rival to know that National would come loaded for that game. He couldn't afford to take a 1–2 team into the final pool-play game with the boys needing to beat their buddies and neighbors just to survive. John had to have a plan to get to 2–1 or 3–0. He needed some breathing room for the guys before the National contest. And what that meant, for John and his staff, was that all roads led back to Scotty.

If Scotty Ringel was on his stride, he could dispatch Berkeley in the first game of the playoffs and still get plenty of rest, almost a week's worth, before returning to the mound to handle Holbrook. Scotty had such a good fastball and such a good off-speed pitch that John felt they had a great chance to beat Holbrook simply by sending Ringel out to throw. The offense would figure something out, but in the meantime Scotty would hold the big bats in check.

Scotty was a little older than the other guys, calmer and more mature, and John was looking for that same normalcy that Scotty was seeking, in part because he had already sensed that the atmosphere surrounding Toms River American wasn't the same in the summer of '07 as it had been the year before. There was a different air around this team. John had been walking a fine line, and he knew it. On the one hand, he had been the one who showed up on the first day of practice and rolled out the Williamsport photo. He was a huge believer in putting the goal right out there, rather than keeping it under wraps or avoiding the topic out of some vague superstition. To John, it was healthy and even encouraging to have such a lofty destination in mind, and to say so out loud.

On the other hand, of course, he was well aware of the pressure that had begun to creep in from almost every direction: from friends, from the other coaches, from parents, and from the town's baseball history itself. The boys, though, seemed somewhat confused about how to feel and act. They didn't know how to be front-runners.

"We started talking about which games we needed to win in order to get to this opponent or that one, thinking way ahead," Vinny said. "Some guys were joking about who would be the stars and who would get interviewed. We had never talked about that stuff the summer before. That year, we might sit there during a game and make little predictions to each other, like, 'I'm predicting Johnny is going to get a hit here.' We weren't even thinking about the next game. But once you start talking about Williamsport, it's hard to talk about anything else."

Though the practices leading up to the tournament were still fast-paced, the boys appeared slightly more laid back. From his position, it struck Scott Ringel almost immediately that the players didn't seem to have quite the same edge they'd had the year before. As 11-year-olds, they had been impressively attentive, using their first exposure to Coach John's methods as a real learning tool. They were, taken together, a quiet bunch. They spent much of the summer of '06 nodding and hustling, and they had the chemistry and desire of a team that hadn't yet realized it could win big games.

By the time the boys got back together in late June of '07, they had a different vibe. They were a little louder, a little more vocal in general. False bravado shot around the practice field, one kid to another. It was as though they had crossed some threshold the year before that entitled them to adopt a slightly different personality, and they were trying on the role of the favorite. It wasn't an approach that made Johnny happy. When he saw all the joking and the laughter, the easy way some of his guys moved through their drills, he wasn't sure his team still had what it took to win. He would have to see the games themselves to know.

He needed to see his team together again, on the field, doing what it did.

"I wonder," Johnny said, "if we want it bad enough."

BY THE TIME SCOTTY TOOK the mound against Berkeley, right there on Toms River's own Little League field, John and his coaches had basically figured out the type of game they were going to have to play in order to win: close, and with not much room for error. The Americans had a little more power than they might have initially thought. Johnny had grown enough as a batter to join Scotty and Quintin as potential home-run hitters, and the surprise of the season was Vinny, another "roll-around 12" closer to age 13, who was hitting balls over fences with a power he had never shown before. John hadn't planned on Vinny being a starter, but there was no keeping him out of the lineup now. The extra offense helped, and John had to take it wherever he could find it. He hoped another run here or there in the games would give him some leeway on what pitchers he used and when he used them—and that, really, was the key to everything.

Scotty had to pitch this first game not only to beat Berkeley, whom John didn't think would score much off him, but to set up the team to face Holbrook the following week with its best lineup—that is, with Scotty on the mound. In the dugout, the Americans all understood the rationale: get the early victory and try to stay on schedule with the pitching rotation. It was just that it felt a little desperate, using Scotty to make sure they beat a likely non-playoff team.

In the stands, Kelly Volk began her usual pacing. Mo's mother was a classic game-time worrier; when it came to sports, she considered herself a gloom-and-doom type, always watching for that trap door underneath first base, or some such. In this case, Kelly had been listening to Mo through the 12 days of workouts leading up to the Berkeley game, and she had formed her own opinion about the team and the boys' chances. Kelly wasn't certain that the kids would get out of pool play in one piece, although she had to admit that her husband, Jerry, sounded pretty confident, and as one of the coaches he was with the kids all the time. But as far as Kelly was concerned, the future was a toss-up until proved otherwise.

All things being equal, Kelly would just as happily stay home during these games. They ate her up. She admired the moxie of some of the other parents, like Billy Sullivan's mother, Kim, who just seemed to stay so relaxed and confident through the innings. Kim liked to camp out beyond the outfield fence with a huge, hand-painted red target, as if to say to Billy and the other Toms River hitters, "Hit it out here." Kim seemed to be having fun with the whole deal— and Kelly envied that. Kelly paced and dealt with her nerves. She did not handle the anxiety well—"the whole what's-gonna-happen thing," as she put it—and so the actual routine of the games was more traumatic than joyful for her.

But Kelly still attended, and she did so for the simple reason that Mo was out there, and this felt like the last year that the Americans had an opportunity to accomplish something genuinely great. Oh, sure, Little League existed beyond age 12; in Toms River, as might be expected, lots of kids still played at the Juniors and Seniors levels, where the bases were moved to 90 feet apart (from the 60 feet that the Americans were playing now) and the mound went back to a regulation 60 feet, 6 inches. The players in Toms River, as they coursed through the intermediate school programs and got ready for high school ball, were always looking for a place to get in a few innings, and Little League continued to fill the bill in that regard beyond this year.

But the 12-year-old season was the most exciting, and the parents understood that. This was the year when you could make it to the regional tournament in Bristol or the World Series in Williamsport and see your children televised on ESPN or ABC. This was the year when heroes were anointed, the way the Gaynors and the Fraziers were for Toms River East back then. It was, in many ways, a finish line, and what lay beyond the finish wasn't particularly appetizing. Stories abounded of the 13-year-old season, when the players continued to play their games, but in front of mostly empty stands and with no special enthusiasm. "I hear about the other parents whose kids are playing Juniors, and how nobody cares," Kelly said. "One mother said, 'Oh, this year's been great. I just drop him off and then go buy groceries.' She'd been to, like, two games. It's kind of sad, really. It's like being an Olympian on the Russian gymnastics team; all of a sudden, you're thirteen, and you're done."

So Kelly wanted to enjoy the ride while she could. She took her place in the outfield bleachers at the Mapletree complex, with Kim Sullivan and Diane Puleo and Donna Gulla and the scads of other parents and friends and fans. She took a deep breath. And then she turned to the field to watch her son's Little League team.

What she saw didn't make her stomach feel any better. If John had wondered how his team was going to handle adversity as a favorite, he didn't have to wait long to get a glimpse: Scotty, the ace of the pitching staff, was in trouble from the start.

The problem wasn't Scotty's stuff; his arm looked fine. He was throwing the ball hard enough. The problem was that the same pitches that baffled so many hitters in 2006 were now getting rocked by the Berkeley batters, who were bigger, stronger and quicker than they had been the year before. Scotty gave up three runs in the first inning, almost before any of the Toms River parents had a chance to take their seats in the stands.

"They came out and let us know what we're in for!" John shouted to his kids as they came running off the field. "We just got started! Let's get the bats going and get back in this thing! Come on, let me hear it!"

But the dugout felt tense, and it was quiet almost as soon as John stopped speaking. The boys, for having chirped so much during practice, didn't have much to say. Scotty looked a little shocked. This certainly wasn't the way he had planned on starting the All-Star season, especially after being the shutout king last summer. He grabbed his batting helmet and walked slowly down to the far end of the dugout, getting ready to hit.

Fortunately, Scotty had a teammate who was ready to step up to the moment. And from the time of his first trip to the plate, in the second inning, Johnny Puleo made it clear that he had come to play.

Johnny's first at-bat announced him. Seeing a fastball

from the Berkeley pitcher, he used his quick hands to whip his bat through the strike zone, and he could feel the perfect contact when he met the pitch. The ball took off on a line and sailed over the right-field fence, a no-doubt-about-it home run. Johnny circled the bases quickly, with his head down, but he could hear the Toms River parents in the stands—and more important, he could hear the guys in the dugout. Johnny could hear Vinny screaming, "Yeah! Yeah! Yeah!" as he came around to score, and when he looked up, his American teammates were out there around home plate, ready to greet him as soon as he touched the base to make the homer official. The boys closed in on Johnny, good-naturedly pounding him on the helmet. John's kid had gotten the blood flowing on the Toms River side.

But the Americans were still in a struggle of a game against Berkeley. By the end of three innings, the Americans were losing 4–1, and John made the difficult decision to pull Scotty in favor of Andrew Hourigan. It was a move made partly because Berkeley was hitting Scotty, and partly because John wanted his best pitcher to be fresh for his next start, two games from now.

"Save it for Holbrook," John told Scotty, rubbing a palm against the pitcher's back.

"Okay," Scotty replied, clearly annoyed with himself for not performing better.

It was the right switch at the right time. Andrew came in throwing an assortment of off-speed pitches, and the Berkeley hitters suddenly looked less sure of themselves. Toms River got out of the fourth inning without giving up any more runs. Now the Americans needed to jolt their offense back to life. Fortunately for them, Johnny was still in the game.

When Johnny came up again in the fourth, Quintin already had doubled and scored on Scotty's single, cutting Berkeley's lead to 4–2. At that point, Johnny didn't figure to see a decent pitch; he assumed the Berkeley pitcher would simply work around him, since he had the home run earlier in the game. He was all the more astonished to see the fast-ball that came, instead, right down the middle.

Johnny swung. Again, he felt the kind of contact that signaled perfect timing. Again, the ball jumped into the sky.

For the second time in two at-bats, Johnny Puleo had hit a home run. This time, he tied the game 4–4, sent the Berkeley pitcher packing and ignited a Toms River rally that produced two more runs—including hits by Austin and Chris Gulla, whose arm didn't hurt when he swung a bat.

In the dugout, John tried to contain his glee; he special-ized in even-keel coaching during the games themselves, never getting too giddy at any one development. But the truth was, he felt the Americans were bound to win as soon as he saw Johnny's second homer go up in the evening sky. And when Johnny came up again in the fifth inning and smashed a two-run double that rolled to the outfield wall, John needn't have bothered to restrain himself. He had the player of the game out there—and the best part was John-ny's demeanor. As he slid into second base with his third hit of the night, having produced five RBIs and given Toms River a comfortable 8–4 lead, Johnny simply bounced up and stared off into the distance, an almost disinterested look on his face. It was a classic head game being played by an experienced All-Star. Johnny gave every indication that he had expected to do what he had just done. He made it look like business as usual.

With that, the Americans relaxed and went back to performing the way they had the summer before. By the time it was over, Toms River had won 11–6, and almost every player in the lineup had produced at least one hit and scored a run. The boys had put the first one in the book. It was not artful, and there was no question that Scotty looked mortal out there on the mound, but a win was a win, especially when it came in the opening game of the tournament.

On the ride home, Johnny proudly sat in silence. He had delivered: two home runs and a long double—he had come close to a three-homer game. The Americans had seen Johnny become a leader right in front of them, a continuation of his development as a top-level player last summer, hit by hit. Now Johnny, a kid so slender-looking and expressionless that opposing pitchers almost always seemed shocked when he blasted their fastballs to the fence, had arrived for the biggest games of his life. Driving back to the house, John pondered his good fortune: His own son was becoming a real player. And just in time.

THE BRICK AMERICAN GAME FOUR days later, on July 1, felt like the official entryway to the Hades of the district tournament. When you came right down to it, the district was a minefield, and dangerous programs like the one in Brick Township—or "Bricktown," as it was often called—always seemed to be just one misstep away from victory. Brick had a long history of fielding competitive teams, but that wasn't even the point this year. The point was that Brick American had a pitcher whom, to hear the story told, almost no one could find a way to hit, and he was headed Toms River's way.

The boy's name was Scott Steimle, and the whispers around him spoke of those 75-mph fastballs, the ones that got in your face in the same amount of time that a Randy Johnson pitch might get to a pro ballplayer. It was said that Steimle threw a no-hitter against another Brick team in their Little League championship series (this was true; Steimle had struck out 15 batters), and that, when he was really throwing his hardest, opposing teams even had trouble trying to bunt. Steimle came throwing heat, and his pitches were difficult to track under the best of circumstances, much less in the high sun of a late-afternoon game. And in one of those developments that John Puleo had been anticipating ever since last summer, Brick American had held Steimle out of its first pool-play game so that he would be fresh to face Toms River at 4 p.m. in Holbrook. Welcome to the world of being the favorite.

Brainstorming for how to prepare, John and Paul Fabricatore at first tried firing pitches at the kids from maybe 20 feet away. It was a marginal exercise at best. The better idea, and the one they finally seized upon, was to call out a player from the past. The Toms River American team of 2005, the one that went all the way to the regional finals, had been filled with good players, but none better than a boy named Kyle Perry, who still worked out at the complex all the time. Kyle was now 14, and he threw much harder than any of the pitchers that the current All-Stars had seen this year. At John's invitation, Kyle agreed to come to the Americans' practice and get on the mound, leaving the All-Stars to try to figure out how to time their swings to connect with fastballs they could barely see. Slowly, painstakingly and with not a few embarrassing cuts along the way, the boys started to clue in. By the day before the game, after two days' worth of Kyle's pitches, John felt that his guys at least had a fighting chance to make contact with Steimle's heat.

Of course, none of that would matter if Toms River couldn't hold Brick's offense in check, especially at a field like Holbrook's where the outfield fences were closer to 180 feet from home plate than the 200 feet that was standard at most Little League parks. Today, it would be Chris Gulla's job to try. After two weeks of severely limited throwing activity, Chris's forearm was feeling considerably better; at the same time, the Gulla family and John both realized that this might be simply because he hadn't been using the arm to throw. John had burned Scotty and Andrew in the Berkeley game, and he needed to have Scotty ready for Holbrook. Beyond that, John still wasn't sure what kind of pitcher Johnny would be when he finally put him out on the mound. The summer before, Johnny had had a couple of nice outings, but he also had gotten hit hard at the state tournament. He had thrown pretty well for the Red Sox during the regular season, but that wasn't against a team full of All-Stars. In John's mind, Johnny probably needed to be the Americans' number three or four pitcher if they were going to make a truly deep run.

So Chris Gulla it was. John's plan was to have Chris

throw mostly fastballs, get comfortable in his pitching motion again, and then slowly work in some off-speed pitches
until Chris felt confident about those, too. The Americans
could use their other pitchers, but John felt drawn to Chris
right now. If he could just get over the hump, maybe throw
a few good innings and walk off with a smile on his face,
the coach thought, then the emotions would lock back into
place. They'd get their old Gulla back. And then the Americans could begin charting the future.

But Chris just wasn't there yet; he was tentative right
from the start. He got out of the first inning without incident, but in the second inning the Brick hitters figured out
that they weren't going to see many changeups or curveballs, and they started waiting for the fastballs that Chris was
almost certain to throw. All of a sudden, balls were shoot-
ing around the Holbrook park and the Toms River coaches
were conferring about what to do.

"He was not on at all," said Donna, Chris's mother. "You
could see that from the stands."

More than that, Chris's body language was all wrong.
Chris pitched almost from a defensive posture, as if he were
bracing himself after each throw—as if he expected his
pitches to get hit.

"He didn't want to be out there," said Scott Ringel.
"You can understand it."

It was hard enough taking the mound in a pressure-
filled game, but right now Chris felt especially vulnerable
because he couldn't throw his pitches the way he'd been
throwing them for the past two years. Between the broken
thumb and the tendonitis, he felt like he was a shell of the

player he had been for John only a year before, and the sense that he might be letting his coach down had begun to creep into him. Almost as soon as the first single whistled off one of the Bricktown bats in the second inning, Chris seemed to give in to a mood of defeat. After a walk, two more hits and a play at home plate in which Chris, trying to cover home and make a tag, got banged into by the sliding baserunner, John knew he had to make a move to save both Chris and the game.

"Not your day, kid," John said to Chris as he walked out to the mound. He looked at the scoreboard. Brick American already had a 3–0 lead, and it was still the middle of the second inning. The coach swallowed hard and did exactly what he had hoped not to do.

"Johnny!" he shouted to his son, who was playing short-stop. "Get in here and pitch."

They were words that chilled John to the bone. Watching Johnny take the mound was one of the few things left in Little League that could reduce John to feeling like a nervous father in the stands. John had coached so many games by now, over so many years, that one might assume he had long since made his peace with the sensation of see-ing his son in a tight situation; but the truth was that Johnny had been such a late bloomer as a pitcher, John had always been able to call somebody else's number instead. Johnny was never the front-liner. Even last summer, John reached out for Scotty or Chris or even Andrew before he tapped Johnny to pitch.

John was self-aware enough to realize that he was, in the moment, simply protecting his son, even if Johnny didn't want or especially need protecting. Maybe John was trying to spare himself and Diane the same agony that the other moms and dads dealt with every time their children were sent out to pitch. It was certainly easier on John's emotions to find someone else to put under that light.

What John didn't know, or was just beginning to learn, was that his son did not share that concern. Johnny Puleo wanted the ball. In Johnny's mind, he had made the transition from a boy who wanted to be a really good baseball player to a boy who knew he was one. Physically, Johnny looked almost identical to the kid who wore the Toms River All-Star uniform in 2006—he hadn't grown much, and he was still about as wide around as a straw—but emotionally, the changes were there. He was ready for the spotlight. He wasn't afraid.

"I got it," Johnny, getting to the mound, told his dad simply.

So he did.

The third run that Brick American got against Chris would be the team's last. Johnny came in and put out the fire immediately. Needing to hold Brick right where it was, Johnny worked his changeup as he warmed up, and he could tell it was going to be an effective pitch for him today. He wasted no time getting it going. The Brick batters, after seeing Chris's steady diet of fastballs, were caught off-balance by Johnny's change in speeds. He got a huge strikeout for the second out of the inning, and then another strikeout to end it. The batters didn't even seem to see his pitches particularly well; they almost lunged at his changeup. "He just took the team on his back," John said. But rather than run gleefully off the mound, Johnny headed for the dugout with the same blank expression he wore as a hitter or an infielder. It was the expression that told the Brick players and fans he was nonplussed by what had just happened.

And because Johnny had figured out how to silence the Brick offense, his Toms River teammates now had time to put a mark on Scott Steimle.

It was Vinny Ignatowicz who finally left that mark—and in almost every way, that was the best possible news. Under-sized for most of his Little League career, Vinny spent the spring in a state of almost constant surprise that his body had finally caught up to his attitude. He had always been good, and he'd always been a talker, but Vinny had never been a power threat. Suddenly, this year, he was hitting line drives that cleared Little League fences—and the distance had little to do with raw strength. It was all about timing. Vinny, by dint of the fact that he had survived for years by putting the ball in play, had become excellent at timing pitches. And as he stood in against Steimle in the third inning, timing was everything indeed.

Steimle's fastball came blasting toward the plate as if shot from a gun—but Vinny was ready. The days of hitting against Kyle Perry were about to pay off. Vinny sped up his swing the way he'd done while facing Kyle, and he had his bat through the strike zone right on time. The contact looked like something out of a Derek Jeter highlight; the ball just took off. Vinny had no doubt about where it was headed. The ball didn't just get over the fence; it went way out of the park. Vinny knew it right away and began to smile. And as the skinny player from Toms River circled the bases, Steimle couldn't stop from cracking a grin himself. The one thing he hadn't counted on was this kid, of all kids, landing an All-Star home run off him.

John was happy for another reason. Sure, Vinny's hit had just altered the tenor of the game, but in the bigger picture, the coach was thrilled that someone other than Scotty or Quintin had delivered a major hit. This could teach the Americans that any one of them was capable of making a huge contribution to an All-Star game—and, thus, that every one of them was responsible to try.

And beyond all that, Vinny's home run seemed to expose Brick's weakness. The message went out that Scott Steimle could be hit, strictly on timing. The homer seemed to briefly rattle Steimle, who hit the very next batter he faced, reserve Clayton Kapp, on the wrist. Clayton could feel his wrist aching; he was afraid that Steimle's pitch had broken a bone. But in a moment, he ran down to first base—and then shocked Brick by stealing second on the next pitch. The Brick players had been caught napping. The Toms River rally was on.

Now Quintin was up, and he followed Vinny's lead. On a Steimle fastball, Q flicked his bat at the pitch and drove a single to the outfield, scoring Clayton to make it 3–2.

In the stands, Kelly Volk and Diane Puleo ramped up the volume of their cheers. The kids in the dugout started walking around, talking animatedly. Scotty Ringel, tall and sinewy, was the next batter, and in that instant, the Brick pitcher looked mortal again. Steimle had lost just a bit of his edge, and with it went some of his concentration, and he threw Toms River's best hitter a very hittable pitch. Scotty didn't miss it. It was a fastball coming in and a moon shot going out, a deep home run beyond the left-center-field fence. Quintin, running hard for third base, relaxed his stride as he saw the ball's trajectory and began jogging home; he waited there for Scotty, a beaming smile on his face. Once again, the Toms River players tumbled out of the dugout for congratulations. This was the second game in a row they had given up the lead early, then made a comeback. Maybe that was what champions did, to keep coming back like that.

The Americans had a 4–3 lead and the momentum. More than that, though, they had Johnny on the mound. That emotionless expression on his face didn't change the rest of the day, and neither did the wicked effect of his changeup on the Brick hitters. Johnny was able to get the strikeouts when he needed them most: one in a key situation in the fourth inning; another in the fifth; two more in the sixth to end the game. He gave up only one hit. It was the best pitching performance anyone could remember him delivering.

For the second game in a row, Johnny had given his team a huge effort at the exact moment it was needed. Johnny had basically won the first game of the playoffs with his bat. He won this one with his arm.

Johnny refused to see himself as the hero, in part because he had spent so much of his baseball-playing life watching guys like Quintin and Scotty come through in the clutch. He knew that their time was coming; it was a matter of days before it was one of those guys whom everybody would be slapping on the back. Johnny had seen them play the hero's role so many times that it had almost become rote. For that matter, he had been watching today when Scotty hit that ball so far off Scott Steimle. Vinny's homer broke the ice, no doubt, but you'd have to say that it was Scotty's blast that broke open everything else. Scotty was just so good in the moment, so good at stepping up with no fear and grabbing a baseball situation by the horns, finding a way to succeed. Johnny loved the fact that, deep down, Scotty didn't seem to care about nerves and had no time for tentativeness. He just went out and played.

SPEAKING WITH HIS PLAYERS ON the field afterward, John tried hard to contain his elation. He didn't want to say too much. John had never been too much for speeches, anyway, and especially not right after a game. He wanted to communicate a simple message quickly, and let the kids get out of there and go home.

"It was the heart you showed that won it," John said. "But let's not have to dig out of a hole every time we play a game. It's hard having to make a comeback every night.

"Go get your rest. Go see your families. Practice tomorrow at the field. You played a great game. And hey! Hey! We're right where we want to be."

The Americans were now 2–0, and it didn't matter how much they had wobbled to get there. It didn't matter that Chris still couldn't pitch, or that they were down 3–0 in each game before making a comeback. They had proved that they could win games when they weren't at their best, and that was valuable knowledge for an All-Star team to have. And the Americans now had the table set the way they wanted it. They had Scotty Ringel ready to pitch to Holbrook's home-run hitters, and by the time they faced Toms River National, they were going to be 3–0 and just taking it easy until the quarterfinals began. They were not the same team as a year ago, no, but they were still getting the job done.

John felt the kids' positive energy. He felt that they were starting to believe they could win again. They looked like they were going to be able to handle pool play. Chris Gulla was going to get better. Johnny was a surprise new weapon. John thought back to that Williamsport photo, and he knew that letting the boys see the object of their desire had been the right move. Just look at how they had responded already.

"We weren't playing great, but we were still winning," Mo Volk said.

"We had all the best kids, and we were winning our games. There was no reason not to think about the World Series," Vinny said resolutely.

"You just never can see what's around the next corner," Mike Gaynor said. And he was the one who should know.

CHAPTER 6

THE LOOK AND FEEL OF A STRUGGLE

THE RAIN CAME BLOWING IN to the Jersey Shore just before the Fourth of July, and it continued through the holiday. The storms screwed up parade plans and scuttled picnics, and it left water on the fields at all the Little League parks in the area. The water changed things. As any Toms River fan could tell you, it almost never changed them for the better.

Before the storm, John had Scotty Ringel ready to pitch against Holbrook. Although he hadn't looked quite himself in Game 1 of the tournament, there was no question in anybody's mind that Scotty could handle the Holbrook guys. He had championship stuff, and that ache to win. And John knew that Scotty wouldn't get cheated on his effort no matter how the game was going, that he'd continue to work hard to the end.

In the practices before the Brick American game, Scotty had been frustrated by his inability to hit some of the hard-thrown pitches that Coach John was delivering at close range. When his father later returned to the field from having helped clean up one of the other TRLL practice areas, the rest of the Americans were gone, but Scotty was waiting at home plate, a bat in his hands. Scott looked at the infield and noticed that the protective practice net in front of the pitching area had been flipped around in order to accommodate Scott's left-handed throws.

"What's up?" Scott asked his son.

"You need to pitch to me some more," Scotty replied, and then tugged on his batting helmet. There was nothing wrong with his game that a few hundred swings couldn't fix.

Scotty still burned like that. Though he excelled in basketball and soccer, baseball was his first love, and it was the game to which he had always been drawn. As one of the older Americans, Scotty felt a stronger connection to Toms River's baseball history than some of his teammates. Maybe it was because his dad was so well versed in the stories of the Gaynor teams, or maybe it was because Scotty himself wasn't much younger than some of the Toms River American players who made it to Bristol in 2005.

"I want our team to be like that team, like our own Toms River team, the twelve-year-olds," Scotty said. "I want to be in their spot and go to Bristol." And once there, Scotty felt that he had a town's worth of baseball memory that suggested Bristol, and the Eastern Regional, did not have to be the final stop on the tour.

First, though, there was the matter of the district tournament in front of him, and he felt well prepared for Holbrook and their big bats. But that was before the rain.

It came quickly on July 3, a classic sudden summer storm. Over in Philly, about 90 minutes away, the big fireworks show after the Hall & Oates concert had to be pushed back more than two hours, to nearly 11:30 p.m. The same system whipped through Ocean County, and it left pools of standing water all over Toms River. The American players wondered how the water would affect the infield at Holbrook, where they were scheduled to play their third game of the tournament on July 5.

The boys quickly got their answer: They weren't going to deal with the water at all, because the game was being rescheduled. After conferring early on game day, District 18 officials declared that the Holbrook-versus-Toms River American contest would be postponed until Saturday, two days later.

And just like that, the defending champions had been set on an entirely new course.

The Saturday start was a nightmare scenario for the Americans, and it left several of the adults visibly upset at the maneuvering. First and foremost, Coach John's team now would have to play three games in three days: the grudge match against Toms River National on Friday night; the makeup game against Holbrook on Saturday morning; and the first game of the eight-team elimination bracket on Sunday at noon. No other team in the district was being asked to play such a ludicrous schedule. No other team was being asked to come up with enough championship pitching to get through three games in three days.

Some of the parents wondered whether the deal had been fixed. "Come on, it's the New York Yankees thing, where they're trying to bring down the one team," one father said. "The anti–Toms River effect is in full swing. Three games in three days, and we're the only team that gets our own league rival in our own pool? You're telling me that's random? Give me a break."

In fact, the pool-play drawings were random, and it was true that the Saturday time slot was one of the few on the schedule that was available for a makeup game. With the single-elimination quarterfinals beginning Sunday, officials needed to get the game in somehow. But the Toms River folks could be forgiven for wondering what was going on. On Thursday evening, the day the Holbrook game had originally been scheduled, anyone driving over to the Little League facility would have been surprised to look at the field itself: It was in almost pristine condition. The infield and pitcher's mound had been covered with a tarp. The outfield had drained well enough that people could walk around out there and play catch. Holbrook players were at the facility, getting some practice swings in the nearby batting cage. It sure looked like a playable ballpark.

"Three games in three days," Scotty said, mulling over the thought. "I knew it was going to be tougher for us, with everybody aiming at us this year and all that. But I didn't expect this."

The schedule switch wreaked havoc on John's pitching plan. Originally, Scotty was going to work Thursday against Holbrook, come in somewhere under 60 pitches, stay off the mound for the required two days, and be ready to work the quarterfinal, elimination game on Sunday. Now the coaches had to figure out how best to deploy Scotty, who was, at that point, their most seasoned and reliable arm, and they also had to construct a plan for getting through the three-day playing binge without breaking any of the new pitching rules. The coaches understood that a pitcher could throw 40 or fewer pitches in a game and only have to rest one day; but this assumed that 40 pitches would get the job done, and that nothing unusual would happen along the way. What were the chances of that?

But John and the coaches had a bigger, more immediate problem, and that was Toms River National itself. The National game, the rivalry game, suddenly had taken on an even more demanding importance, because a loss would dramatically alter the landscape. The Americans didn't want to be sitting with a 2–1 record when they went to face Holbrook on Holbrook's own field.

John already knew that the National game was going to be an emotional one, but he had originally hoped that at least it wouldn't have playoff implications. That was then. In the here and now, the Americans needed to get to 3–0 to cross over safely to the playoffs, and it was their own intra-league opponent that stood in the way.

FROM THE BEGINNING, THAT NATIONAL game had the look and feel of a struggle. It was like glancing in the mirror and seeing your opposite, for one thing. While the Americans wore their traditional red vests and blue undershirts with their red ballcaps, the National boys had their uniforms flip-flopped: blue vests, red sleeves, blue hats. With both teams wearing white pinstriped pants, Gary

A. Scavuzzo Field at the Mapletree complex took on the appearance of a delayed Independence Day celebration all its own.

The atmosphere had an All-American flavor—if you didn't count the part about the families of the two teams barely acknowledging one another as they walked to their respective bleachers before the game. This had become something of a grim tradition, the parents from the same Little League dividing into two disparate groups. At one point, Chris Gulla's grandfather set up a folding chair near the National stands because it was easier for him to walk to the parking lot afterward. Donna approached him and said gently, "We can't sit here," and proceeded to move him over to the other side of the field. It was simply a case of not looking for a reason to have a problem. It was the smart move.

The outside air was cool, a welcome and sudden relief. The rain had dropped temperatures down into the seventies by evening. The storm had left behind some moisture in the air, and a faint breeze pushed across the outfield. All in all, it was almost comfortable. Everyone understood it wouldn't last.

The two Toms River Little League teams had over the years achieved a natural rivalry, not a forced one. The league's regular-season system, under which Majors division teams were allowed to keep the kids they drafted until they moved on to Juniors, encouraged the formation of clans. If you were picked by, say, the Diamondbacks as a 10-year-old, then you were a member of the D'Backs—and, by extension, a National Leaguer—for the next three years. When

John Puleo drafted Quintin to the Red Sox way back when, that was that. Q was with the Red Sox until he aged out of Majors. He was an American League guy.

A competitive hardening of the arteries occurred over the years, too. There was excellent coaching in both divisions, but it was the American All-Stars who had finally broken through in '05 with all those wins and the run to Bristol, and no one forgot that. Even if you wanted to, the league wouldn't hear of it: Following the lead of East Little League across town, TRLL had constructed signs to commemorate its All-Star teams' successes, and so the names of the 2005 team hovered above the entrance to Scavuzzo Field.

The run-up to this specific game had an edge. Some of the American players told of looking up during their Mapletree workouts to see National players in the bleachers, looking on. And why not? The Nationals wanted to leave their own mark—it was their 12-year-old season, too—and they had talent. They were also hungry: After winning their first two games to begin the All-Star tournament, they had dropped a tough, one-run decision to Berkeley. Now they had a 2–1 record in pool play, and it already seemed clear, looking at the standings, that at least one of the teams that finished 2–2 was not going to move on to the quarterfinals. The Nationals didn't want it to be them. They had to beat the Americans to remove any doubt about making the play-off round.

John, for his part, had to think ahead. The Holbrook postponement had ruined everything he had planned, and he now had to recalibrate his options, especially where the pitching was concerned. Three games in three days? John couldn't think of a team in the district that could put great pitching out there three days in a row. At some point, he had to hope for the best.

Finally, John chose Andrew to pitch against National. It was a calculated move. Andrew had been throwing well, and the sense was that the Americans knew how to hit against the National pitchers. John wanted his offense to rack up some early runs and give Andrew a nice cushion to work with, possibly allowing the boy to go six full innings—or anything close to a complete game, really. If John lost Andrew as a pitcher for three days—that is, if Andrew went above 60 pitches, which he was almost certain to do just to reach the fourth inning or more—but the Americans won, then it was a useful move. They could afford to use some of their second-tier pitchers against Holbrook, and save Scotty for Sunday's opening game of the playoffs. But if they lost to Toms River National, the math of the tournament would change for the worse. The scramble would be on.

Beyond that consideration, Andrew was one of John's true competitors. In the dugout, with his teammates by his side and one of them at bat, he was one of the great cheerleaders of the group; he piped up so vocally and so often that John had taken to calling him Squeaky. Andrew was the one you could hear before you even got to the field, as he'd be leading the team in a group shout-out in between the opposing pitcher's deliveries to home plate. "I'm fired up! You fired up?" Andrew screamed, with his teammates quickly responding in unison, "Yeah!" until the thing took on a steady cadence: I'm-fired-up-you-fired-up-yeah! I'm-fired-up-you-fired-up-yeah! Under Little League rules, the players were told to fall silent when the pitcher got ready to throw, and so the games themselves became exercises in these rising and suddenly falling volumes. Andrew's volume was something to be counted on.

But in action, Andrew was more like Scotty and Johnny. He was as emotionally stable as anyone John had ever coached, and John had had Andrew with him on the Red Sox. Like Scotty and Johnny, Andrew was a "roll-around 12"; he'd already turned 13 by the time he would take the mound on Friday night against Toms River National. He had mastered the art of appearing impenetrable in the field, with no discernible expression crossing his face. If you had just hit a home run off him, you'd never be able to tell it, and if Andrew had just doubled into the gap off you, he would simply slide into second, bounce up and dust himself off, as if he had expected to be there all along. Andrew specialized in getting ready for the next play.

He was human, though, a young man of terribly high self-expectation. In the 2006 tournament, Andrew had drawn a pitching assignment for the section final against Allentown, which was coming out of the loser's bracket and would have to beat Toms River twice to win it all. John was holding back Scotty in case he was needed for the finale, and so Andrew took the mound in a tight game. Despite pitching well, he gave up two runs late, and lost. The performance became moot the next day, with Scotty pitching a shutout for the title and Andrew contributing several defensive gems in the infield. It was a happy ending. But Andrew's father, Tom, never forgot his son's expression after taking the loss on the mound.

"He was *crushed*," Tom said, "and he's normally pretty upbeat, a happy-go-lucky person. But he felt so personally responsible for letting everybody down."

Now, against National, his teammates wanted to give him all the support he needed—and Andrew was happy to contribute to that effort, too. The first batter of the game, Andrew stepped in and carefully worked the count, fouling off a couple of pitches. Finally he drew a walk. One batter later, Quintin stepped into a 1–1 fastball and smacked it on a line over the left-center-field fence, out near where Billy Sullivan's mom was standing with that target sign. The Americans had a 2–0 lead before Andrew had even thrown a pitch.

In their familiar dugout at the Mapletree complex, the boys reveled in the early lead. Finally, they were ahead to begin a game. They had Andrew going out there to pitch, and perfect conditions for a nighttime game in Toms River. It all set up the way they wanted.

It also didn't last. And before long, John was making a decision that he absolutely didn't want to make.

From the start, Andrew was just slightly off his game on the mound. He was throwing about as hard as he usually did, but he was uncharacteristically missing his spots. When Ryan called for an outside fastball, Andrew's pitch came back toward the middle of the plate—and the National hitters knew Andrew well enough to jump all over fat strikes like that. He got through the first two innings without allowing a run, but anyone could see that he didn't have his best stuff.

Then things became ominous. After getting the first two

outs in the second inning, Andrew suddenly lost his control and walked two straight batters on pitches that weren't even close. He worked the next hitter to a full count and then walked him, too, loading the bases. He just couldn't close the deal. He escaped by getting the next batter to pop up, but his wildness had cost Andrew a slew of extra pitches, many more than he should have thrown. It was a worrisome sign.

It blew apart completely not long after. The Americans pushed their lead to 3–0 in the top of the third on a run-scoring fly ball by Johnny, but Andrew continued to misfire on the mound. The National bats heated up, and National took a 5–3 lead by scoring five times in the third—a sort of classic Little League rally, where a couple of walks led to a couple of hits and, before anyone knew it, that many runs already had crossed the plate. But the worst of it was that Andrew was finished for the night on the mound. He had nothing left in his arm; he had thrown too many pitches to go longer than three innings. Coach John was going to have to improvise.

The decision he wound up making owed considerably to what happened next. Drew Fanara, one of the two new faces on the American roster from the year before, was substituted into the game in the top of the fourth to get a turn at bat, and he came up in a critical situation: runners at second and third and no outs, thanks to Ryan's walk and a double by Pauly. It was Drew's turn to shine, and he sliced a double to the right-field fence, scoring two runs to tie the game 5–5—and leading John to realize that this contest was going to be a back-and-forth battle to the final out. The realization changed John's thinking: he was now playing for the win one run at a time, trying to scrape out a survival victory rather than wait for a big rally. He ordered Andrew to bunt Drew to third base, into easy scoring position, and Drew came home with the go-ahead run when Quintin delivered a clean single to center field, the kind of clutch, two-out hit that the Americans had come to expect from Q. They were back on top, 6–5—and John had a decision to make.

In the moment, he decided to go for it.

"Get Scotty warmed up!" the coach said.

Enough with the drama; John wanted Scotty out there on the mound to nurse this victory home and get the Americans to a 3–0 record. Forget Scotty pitching against Holbrook. John would worry about that team tomorrow.

But John was taking a secondary risk. If Scotty threw 40 or fewer pitches against National, he would still be eligible under Little League rules to start the Saturday playoff game on the mound for his team—but if he exceeded 40, then he would be ordered to take an extra day of rest. The Americans wouldn't have Scotty for their first elimination game.

John decided he couldn't dwell on that now. This game, the National game, was the one his team had to win. There could be no going to Holbrook tomorrow morning with a rivalry loss hanging over the boys' heads. You just couldn't play winning baseball that way.

The coach was grinding in a way that he hadn't found himself grinding for a while. He was arguing calls with the home-plate umpire, Burt, who was also a Toms River Little League ump during the regular season. Burt had no business working this game; it was a bad decision by the district officials. He should have been umpiring somewhere else on this night. Burt knew the two managers far too well; that kind of familiarity led to hair-trigger arguments in heated games like these. And he hadn't counted on John's suddenly uneven demeanor.

John generally tried to stay out of confrontations with umpires because of the bad example it set for the kids, but on this night, he was not immune to the pressure. At the end of that fourth-inning rally, Quintin was thrown out trying to score on a wild pitch, a close play on which he appeared from the third-base angle to have slid in under the tag. It was the second time in the game that a play at home had gone against his team, and John became unglued. He rushed in to argue.

"That's twice you've missed that call!" John shouted.

"Go to the dugout, coach," Burt shot back.

"When are we going to get that call? He's under the tag. He's under the tag!"

"Coach, not another word," the umpire said, the anger rising in his voice. "Not another word! Not one more word!"

John retreated to the dugout, then stood there glaring at Burt. On any other day, in the same situation, the coach either would have shrugged off the out call or consciously chosen to let the incident pass. But this was not another night. John started to come out of the dugout again, only to check himself—he knew better than to make a scene, and he had already let the umpire know that John thought he blew the call. There was no point in repeating himself now. The only thing on John's mind, really, was that 7–5 looked a lot better than 6–5, and it had been worth arguing for. Burt seemed to understand; after heatedly shouting down John, the umpire, too, took a minute to cool off, standing over near the backstop.

In the bleachers, one parent turned to the other and smiled.

"Well," he said, "that's the rivalry for you."

But it was more than that. To John, the season was suddenly in the balance. Everything had changed over the past couple of days. The National game wasn't just a win-or-lose proposition; it had implications for everything that was to follow.

"I was so intense in that game," he said afterward. "I wanted that game for the kids. I was not about to let any kind of advantage slip away or go to the other side."

Putting Scotty on the mound wasn't just a decision, then; it was *the* decision. This one simply had to turn out the right way.

But Scotty was still a kid. He was bound to have his human moments like everyone else. Entering the game to pitch, he had one: After getting ahead in the count 1–2, he left a pitch out over the plate and gave up a solo home run, allowing National to tie the game at 6–6. It became evident that this one was going to go all the way to the sixth inning to be decided; there would be nothing clean or simple about it. Looking at the National fans cheering on their hitters, celebrating the tie and trying to encourage their kids to come up with something great, you could understand why John Puleo felt moved to rush the umpire and argue a play at home plate—argue a Little League call, that is. A single run might well decide the game, and with it his team's chances in the tournament.

Scotty avoided trouble in the fifth inning, but the Americans weren't able to score, either. The teams went into the final inning tied, and they were playing slow. The evening was growing long, with the time now edging toward nine p.m. Scotty had found his rhythm on the mound, and he was setting down the National hitters, keeping his team in the game. Now the Americans needed to get a fire going on offense.

And again, Drew Fanara provided a spark. This time up to bat, Drew saw a pitch sailing inside and toward him, and he deftly turned his body away, exposing his back and shoulder to the ball and getting hit by it. Drew could tell that it was coming, and he could tell that, if he moved just so, he could cause the pitch to hit him. Whether or not it would hurt was irrelevant; Drew had gone through enough of John's practices to understand that such was simply expected of him. He was awarded first base, then applauded by the American parents for, essentially, getting hit. It was all part of the mathematics of winning.

Andrew quickly bunted Drew to second, which brought Vinny to the plate with a chance to give his team the lead. And again, Vinny was equal to the challenge. With a smooth swing and solid contact, he grounded a ball right up the middle; the ball bounced over second base and into center field. Drew, running on the contact of the bat, came steaming around third and scored easily, and the Americans had regained the lead at 7–6.

They also were about to receive a gift. Quintin followed with a single to get Vinny to third, and then Q stole second base; but Scotty took a called third strike—a rarity, in that he was almost never caught looking at a good pitch. When Johnny then came up and lifted a routine fly ball to center field, the inning looked over.

But the night came into play. Johnny's pop-up had enough height that it crossed directly in front of the flood-lights that surrounded Scavuzzo Field. Against that bright white light, the ball disappeared from view for an instant. It fell untouched to the grass in shallow center field—the fielder never saw it after it went up in the air—and with both runners going full speed around the bases because there were already two outs, they both scored. What should have been the third out of the inning instead became a two-run "single." The Americans pounded hands against the dugout fence and whooped and hollered, watching their lead balloon to 9–6. Surely that would be all Scotty would need.

What John dearly wanted was for Scotty to throw about three pitches, get three quick outs and run into the dugout with both the victory and his pitch-count safely intact. The problem was, Scotty was not superhuman, and he picked the wrong time to return to earth.

The first batter Scotty faced in the bottom of the sixth was Tommy Zerba, a good-hitting National player whom the American kids knew well. Scotty was working, grinding. He got two strikes on Tommy, but he just couldn't put him away; and finally Tommy found a pitch he could drive. The liner sailed over the fence for a home run to make it 9–7, and the Nationals sprang to life again.

There was no getting around it: Scotty was going to have to work. And John and the coaches were going to have to watch.

The next hitter tried to lay down a bunt, but Scotty hustled over to the ball and threw the runner out at first. One down. The following batter hit a shot that glanced off a diving Johnny's glove and trickled into the outfield for a single, driving the National parents into a frenzy—but Scotty recovered to strike out the following hitter, and now it was the American parents doing the screaming and whooping. The whole inning seemed to rock back and forth on an emotional pivot, swinging from one batter to the next. In the bleachers, both sets of fans were on their feet, cheering the game to its conclusion. On the field, you could see the American players locked into their defensive positions, trying to be ready to pounce on any ground ball or pop-up. Scotty was laboring. He was really pushing hard to the finish. He needed so badly secure this important victory.

And, finally, he got it: a ground ball to Johnny at short-stop. Johnny fielded the ball cleanly and fired a strike across the infield to first base. The umpire's hand went up to signal the third out. The Toms River Americans poured from the dugout and ran in from the outfield, ready to congratulate one another and savor the achievement of a 3–0 record; but a different scene slowly began to emerge. As the American players lined up to shake hands with their National rivals, the emotional drain of the game was written on their faces. They looked spent. It was past nine thirty; by the time they held a postgame meeting and packed up their gear, it would be going on ten o'clock. The Holbrook game was set for ten the next morning, meaning the kids were going to have to get to the Mapletree complex before 9 a.m. for batting practice. It was a severely quick turnaround, considering the scope of the game they'd just played.

John, still slightly embarrassed by his outburst at the umpire and fully aware of the late hour, spoke to the kids briefly.

"We dodged a bullet there," he said. "But great work, great work. Hey, three-and-oh, three-and-oh. Go home and sleep fast."

Then he stepped away, letting the guys meet up with their parents and head over to get drinks at the concession stand. John wanted to join them, maybe soak up the atmosphere for a few minutes; but his mind already had begun to spin ahead to tomorrow and the playoffs beyond. Unbeknownst to all but perhaps the coaches, Toms River's chances had just been dramatically affected.

It was a simple matter of looking in the scorebook. Right there, next to Scotty's name, was the number of pitches he had thrown against Toms River National. The number was 45, and that was five pitches too many.

The Little League national rules on pitch counts were clear. The fact that Scotty had gone past 40 throws tonight meant that he was not eligible to pitch in a game again until he had had at least two days of rest. He could play, but he couldn't pitch. And because of the rain makeup against Holbrook, John Puleo's team was now required to play two games in those two days. The Americans now had to try to win each of those games without their big ace on the mound.

Using Scotty against the Nationals had been the right idea, for this victory sealed the Americans' spot in the playoffs. Now John's team didn't absolutely have to beat Holbrook tomorrow just to survive and advance. But losing Scotty, even for two days, was a problem. He was so clearly the best kid on the mound lately; as good as Johnny had looked, John didn't consider his son in the same category as Scotty when it came to pitching. The idea all along had been to set up the pitching rotation so that Scotty could start the first playoff game, because that was when John felt his kids would be their most nervous—that first real test in the year after their championship run. Now there would be no such security blanket.

The situation with Scotty came down to those five pitches by which he went over the limit. There was no choice about it at the time; it felt like a game the Americans had to close out, after they had worked so hard to regain the lead against their rivals. But a price had been paid.

Now John had to reconsider his strategy. He had to reconsider Chris Gulla, and maybe Johnny, too. He had to figure out how to approach Holbrook's big hitters, and with whom. As Scotty had just proved, there were no sure things out there; even with the elite kids, it was tricky. The Toms River boys now were one day away from the point at which every inning, every pitch became a critical step along the road they wanted to travel. They were just beginning to discover how long the road could be.

SATURDAY MORNING ARRIVED SUNNY AND hot, and it arrived quickly. For the Americans, it also arrived with the distinct feel of a baseball hangover. The guys had gotten home late, tried to go to bed as quickly as possible—

and, being 12 and 13 years old, failed spectacularly at fall-ing asleep right away. Walking onto the Mapletree field for some pregame batting practice, Quintin smiled the sheepish smile of a kid who was still trying to wake up. Johnny and Scotty were even more reserved than usual. The whole scene seemed to play out through a fog.

The guys all knew that, technically, they didn't have to beat Holbrook to advance, which was always a terrible mind-set to take to the baseball diamond. Unquestionably, a 4–0 record would be better than 3–1, because it meant drawing the lowest-seeded team from the other pool in Sunday's first round—and Johnny, for his part, wanted that fourth win for precisely that reason.

"You want the number-one seed, so you can play the worst team left in your pool," he said. "The low seed is the team that had the most trouble so far. That's the team we want right now."

John agreed with the theory, but the previous game's events had overtaken such simple math. John had to calcu-late just how much energy the team could afford to spend on the Holbrook game. Anyway, to John's thinking, District 18 was so stacked with quality Little Leagues that once a team advanced to the quarterfinals, there really were no easy games left. It was a matter of tough versus tougher, that's all.

The Toms River players were running on empty, with no emotional reserve in the tank. Physically, this was a group that had gone nearly two months straight in 2006 without falling apart; but the game against Toms River National had had an obvious effect, which was spread among the players, the par-ents and even the coaches a bit. Getting that win had felt so huge. Here on Saturday morning, not even 12 hours after that game had ended, the fallout was obvious.

Scott Ringel dropped Scotty off at the field, parked the car in the Mapletree lot and walked over. Even from afar, Scott could detect the low energy level, and he knew the National game had left a mark. "Those kinds of games around here are so big," he said. "They were so determined not to lose to National, their own rivals. That was a tough game in general, let alone having to stage a rally to win it. Those games are just tough."

John's view was that beating National did take some of the urgency out of the Holbrook game. He had some options, and he picked one of them: It was going to be Pauly on the mound. John usually spoke to his coaches to gauge their opinions on roster decisions, but he did not believe in a management-by-committee approach to the game. This time he made the call on Pauly by himself, and he didn't ask for feedback.

Pauly was hardly an unknown quantity on the mound; he had pitched well against the Red Sox enough times over the years for John to know all about him. And John had high confidence in Pauly anytime that his knuckleball was working, because it was the kind of pitch that might baffle hitters for an entire game, or at the least for a few innings. The concern with Pauly was strictly endurance; he was, in some ways, still recovering from his season with the Rangers, when he had pitched so much that he arrived at All-Star practice with a tired arm. But John could play that by ear. The upside was obvious: If Pauly was on, and holding Holbrook at bay, John might just ride the hot hand and see how far Toms River could go.

The ideal result was to beat Holbrook without using a pitcher from the "A" category, a group that now included only Johnny and Chris, since neither Scotty nor Andrew was available under the rules. Pauly Schifilliti, when he was good, was very, very good. If he could work more than a couple of innings—that is, if his arm held up—then the Toms River team was going to be in great shape for the stretch run to the district finals.

The real wild card was the Holbrook team itself; and as the Americans and their parents pulled into the parking lot at the Holbrook Little League complex and walked to their side of the field, they suddenly understood why. For weeks, the buzz around the district's Little Leagues was that the Holbrook lineup looked different than it ever had before, and now Vinny, getting out of his dad's car, saw the evidence for himself.

"They're huge," Vinny said. "They look like they're twice the size we are. I don't know what happened over there, but I can tell you this: We didn't grow, and they did."

It was true. Several of Holbrook's kids appeared to have hit their growth spurts at the same time, while only Scotty among the Toms River players had really experienced a significant physical change. This was one of the few elements over which neither coach nor player had any control. In 2006, the Americans looked to be a team of roughly average size. Here in '07, as Vinny put it, "We look small."

BY THE TIME THE BOYS took the field at Holbrook on the morning of July 7, the heat was beginning to radiate, and the fans were ready for some baseball. Holbrook's crowd was almost always dependably large and loud, and the folks had good reason to get rowdy on this day: their All-Star team had outscored the opposition 28–5 in its first three pool-play games. This game was, for Holbrook, a chance to get a few digs at Toms River after the past several years of playing third or fourth fiddle in the district, behind both Toms River and Jackson.

And from the beginning, the day had an uneasy feel about it. The weather couldn't seem to decide whether to go full-blown humid or ease off and cut the patrons a break, and so it hovered between hospitable and hostile. Kim Sullivan, Billy's mom, headed for the outfield bleachers to hold up her painted target, but at the last minute she was told by Holbrook officials that the sign had to be folded up and put away—something about it being a distraction to the players. Since Kim held up the sign only when the Toms River boys were batting, it was hard to figure exactly where the distraction lay, but Kim was so surprised by the command that she simply put the sign away, shaking her head.

"I've held that thing up everywhere we've been," she said, a look of bemusement crossing her face. "But not at Holbrook, I guess."

She could tell this wasn't going to be a friendly visit. The Holbrook fans had waited a while for their boys to get this competitive, and they had the feeling that this might be their year. They were already 3–0 in pool play, and they looked dominant. The Americans had achieved the same record without blowing anyone away. Maybe the kids from the "baseball town" had used up all their excellence the summer before. This was one chance, the first chance, for Holbrook to find out.

Pauly Schifilliti felt like he was up for that challenge. His arm may not have been at its liveliest, but despite his season of pitching deep and repeatedly in games, he didn't feel exhausted. And with his knuckleball, Pauly was uniquely built among the Toms River pitchers to deal with Holbrook's fastball-hitting behemoths. His job was going to be to keep his team in the game by keeping Holbrook in the park, so to speak. Home runs had to be limited.

As it turned out, Pauly gave up home runs in each of the first two innings, but those were mistakes, fastballs in the strike zone that John called for and that Pauly realized (after the fact) he shouldn't have thrown. Otherwise, if you were Toms River, you had to like what you were seeing. Pauly's knuckleball was doing its dance; the big Holbrook hitters were having trouble staying patient at the plate. He might just survive the assignment.

And the Americans, while clearly not sharp as a team, were getting by in roughly the same manner. Andrew led off the bottom of the first with a single, and Vinny scored him with a double to the fence between right and center field. Scotty added a two-out, two-strike single to score another run, and it was 2–2. When Vinny came through again in the bottom of the third, driving a homer deep to left field, the tired, emotionally drained Toms River team had somehow woken up in time to be right in this game. It was a 3–3 score after three innings, and even if Johnny, at shortstop, had the distinct feeling that his team wasn't completely there that day, they were in a real, live contest.

And then they weren't. And after that, it got worse. And at some point that Saturday afternoon in Holbrook, it became hard to remember that the team from Toms River was the defending district champ.

What happened was simple: John replaced Pauly on the mound. Pauly was creeping up above the 50-pitch mark, and John wanted to make sure Pauly didn't overthrow or put much of a strain on his arm. In addition, this game didn't count the way the next few games were going to count. It certainly wasn't worth trying to extend Pauly into dangerous territory, and, for that matter, the coaches all knew they'd be using at least two pitchers that day from their second tier of guys, simply to spread out the innings, get a couple of players their work on the mound, and stay sharp for the playoffs.

Pauly, though, walked away confused. He felt he was doing a good job, and he wasn't in any pain. Holbrook had actually been a team that some of the Toms River kids had worried about, but with Pauly on the mound it looked like a winnable game.

"He didn't say anything to me—he just took me out," Pauly said. "I didn't agree with it and I didn't understand it.

"I could have kept going. I think I could have done a good job out there."

As the team headed to the field to begin the top of the fourth, Pauly stayed in the dugout. He shook his head slowly as he watched Billy Sullivan go to the pitcher's mound to warm up. Billy had looked good as he loosened up in the bull pen, and he had had several good practice sessions in recent days. His left-handed delivery was loose and easy, which fit his personality perfectly: Billy didn't worry about much, and he seemed to more or less enjoy all the baseball he played. His mom, Kim, was the fun one. The Sullivans always seemed to know how to keep it relaxed.

But standing in right field, Vinny felt a sudden twinge in his gut. He knew that Billy threw almost all fastballs, and he knew that the Holbrook kids had been sitting at the plate waiting for fastballs to come. One reason Pauly had messed them up was that he would nibble around, change speeds, throw a lot of junk. It was Pauly's fastballs that got hit over the fence. And now here came Billy with more fastballs. It just didn't add up.

As it was, it added up plenty. Billy got started, and within three batters the mood of the game had undergone a sea change. The Holbrook batters got that look in their eyes, and they started smacking line drives; and then one of the big kids, Brendan Benecke, hit a huge shot over the fence, just a monster home run. The Holbrook parents came alive, bellowing and braying from their side of the field. Johnny waited for his dad to go get Billy off the mound; anyone could see that Billy didn't have it. But John had already made his decision. He wasn't going to lose another valuable pitcher before the real playoffs began.

In what seemed like two minutes' time, Holbrook was ahead 6–3, and then 8–3, and then 10–3. Billy couldn't keep the Holbrook hitters in the park. From his spot in the dugout, John spoke to Billy only occasionally, encouraging him to continue throwing strikes—which Billy obviously was doing, since they were being hit for home runs.

"Baseballs were flying," said Scotty.

It was a small field, anyway, with those 185-foot fences. Billy was throwing strikes, and Holbrook turned out to be just as strong and as offensive-minded as it had appeared. John saw the trouble, but the game got out of hand so quickly that even a rapid pitching change might not have made much difference.

For that matter, John knew the situation. Scotty and Andrew were unavailable. Johnny and Chris were off-limits because of the pending playoff game tomorrow. Pauly was already out of the game, a mistake that John couldn't undo now. Realistically, the pitchers who might come in to re-place Billy would be guys without much game experience on the mound, and certainly without All-Star type experi-ence. When John added it up, it was a pretty ugly equation no matter which way he looked at it.

And so Billy stayed. John didn't worry about what to say to him, because he knew Billy well and felt that, of all his players, Billy could handle the emotional fallout the best.

"Keep throwing," John said from the dugout. "Those are good strikes. You're doin' fine."

The message was clear: Billy was going to take one for the team. He was remarkably composed about it. If he was frustrated, his face belied none of it. There were no tears, just an occasional shaking of his head as he watched another ball fly out of the park. Billy wasn't really a big-time pitcher, after all; he was just doing what Coach John needed him to do. When it was over, Billy knew, he would go back to the outfield positions that he played so well, and he would go back to playing like the All-Star he was. But for the time be-ing, he was going to have to try to get through the drubbing if he could.

Watching Billy stay out there, the Toms River parents

grew quiet in the stands; they could see what was happening, and there was nothing at all to do about it. Kim Sullivan, the handmade target she had brought sitting folded in her lap, looked on without comment. Like her son, she understood the deal. And Billy's sacrifice was as terrible as it sounded. To watch it was, on several levels, just plain shocking. The Holbrook kids pounded hit after hit. Brendan Benecke smashed his second homer of the day in the fourth inning, a shot that went over everybody's head, even the parents scattered under the few shade trees beyond the outfield fences. The Holbrook fans were delirious, then amazed, and finally quiet, as if they realized this was no longer a competitive Little League game.

John eventually brought in both Vinny and Quintin to pitch a little, but it couldn't have mattered less. The Holbrook kids were venting, and they were slugging, and it was a home-run derby. Sitting in the outfield seats, Donna Gulla saw one homer fly past her on such a firm trajectory that she found herself turning all the way around, watching to see where the ball would come down. "It landed at about second base on the field behind us," she said.

The game ended there, in the fourth, after the explosion finally finished and the Toms River guys came to bat and made three quick outs. Holbrook's victory was by an 18–3 score, and, by the count of the coaches, eight home runs. It was like watching the varsity take on the junior varsity. It said *Toms River* on the other players' uniforms, but that was no defending district champion over there. Even the winners found it almost strange to watch the reigning champs get so thoroughly trashed—and it went well beyond Billy. The fielders behind him had been uniformly awful, kicking routine grounders, failing to cover the base on plays, missing the cutoff men with their throws. They had experienced a collective meltdown.

"It wouldn't have mattered if we'd had Tom Seaver on the mound," John said later. "We didn't have it, and Holbrook tore us up."

The coach said it matter-of-factly, but it wasn't that easy. For the pros, maybe, a loss like that was something you could just throw away, but among the Toms River American kids, the first signs of a crack began to show. "We'd never been beaten anything like that," Pauly said. "That was totally new to us."

A few kids laughed at the scene after a while; it was so hideous, laughing was all you could do. Johnny grew more and more sullen; he felt embarrassed to be out there getting trashed like some chump team from one of the crummy Little Leagues. He was from Toms River, for cripes' sake. He was from the district and section champ. Sure, Billy had turned out to be the wrong pitcher that day, but that was no excuse for Johnny or anyone else to start acting like a third-grader in the field.

And Johnny was angry for another reason. Just like the coaches, Johnny liked to keep the numbers in his head, and he knew exactly what this loss was going to mean. Toms River would finish in second place in Pool A, behind unbeaten Holbrook, and tomorrow the Americans were going to have to play Manchester rather than Brick National in the first round of the playoffs. Both of those teams had 3–1 records, but Manchester was the higher seed and a much stronger club. The Brick team hadn't beaten anybody good in pool play; its 3–1 record still left it as the fourth out of four seeds in the pool. It was every bit to Holbrook's advantage to finish 4–0 and get Brick in that first round, and Holbrook had just played this game as if it had had everything to gain. Johnny was frustrated and angry that not enough of his teammates cared to do the math with him; if they had, they would have scratched and clawed and done everything they could to win, instead of throwing the game out the window like a wadded-up piece of gum.

If pounding the Americans into the ground wasn't sufficient, the Holbrook coaches had gone one further: They had one of their baserunners steal home on a wild pitch—to make the score 14–3—in that fourth inning. "We had beaten them pretty bad the year before," John said, "so maybe they had an ax to grind." In reality, though, the coaches may just have wanted to make sure the game would end when they wanted it to. Little League "run rules" allowed for a game to be stopped after four innings if one team was beating the other by 10 or more runs; by scoring that 14th run, Holbrook was trying to give itself a slight cushion going into the bottom of the fourth, in case Toms River scored a run. Holbrook was no longer worried about getting the win, but there was significant value in not having to use a pitcher over the final two innings of a game.

Toms River had just gotten trashed. The news quickly spread around the district, traveling by word of mouth from one coach to another, from parent to parent. Never had a defending champion looked more vulnerable.

John was determined to keep some perspective. The entire game came down to one horrible inning by the Americans, and the coach felt it was a good, tight contest otherwise.

But John could see in the eyes of his players that something bad had happened here. There were looks of confusion, even among his top-shelf guys. He could tell that Johnny was smoldering. Several of the other boys were staring straight down at the dugout floor.

"You have to forget that one," John told the kids. "It didn't count. It goes like that sometimes. Just go on home, be with your families. Get some rest. Take the rest of the day and go enjoy it."

He looked around at his team, the one he had practically handpicked. These were John's All-Stars. They were good Toms River kids, and he knew the pressures they were carrying. He wasn't going to add to them.

"We'll win tomorrow, and then we'll get set for the rest of the week," John said. He said it because he believed it. He had seen so many cases of a team performing badly one game and then roaring back to form the next; it almost always depended upon having the stars in the right spots on the field. And John still had a star that he had been keeping in his pocket. He had protected Chris Gulla for long enough. It would be so good finally to see that star shine.

CHAPTER 7

SIX GOOD INNINGS

JOHN DIDN'T GIVE CHRIS THE news until the team had gathered at the Mapletree complex for batting practice on Sunday morning, July 8. He could have told Chris the day before that he would be the starting pitcher against Manchester, but there was no upside to doing so. At this age, the kids certainly didn't train or eat differently depending upon what position they were going to play the next day; for the most part, they ate what they wanted and had to be told by their parents to quit playing PlayStation, shut off the lights and get some sleep. They did the same things that they always did. All John might accomplish by telling Chris on Saturday would be a premature set of frayed nerves.

Though he knew he should be excited, Chris didn't know quite what to feel when Coach John pulled him aside to give him the news. Chris knew that he wasn't completely recovered from the tendonitis, because his performance against Brick American had been so shaky. He figured that

Coach John had to be a little desperate to be sending him out there, especially after what had happened in Holbrook the day before, but the way that John put it was so encouraging that Chris found himself wanting to change his own mind. Maybe his coach was putting him out there because he really did believe what he told Chris, that Chris was too good *not* to pitch in this game.

"There's no one I would rather have on the mound today," John said. "You can do this. You're a great pitcher. Just go do what you do, and you'll be fine."

Having Chris on the mound allowed John to set the defense the way he wanted. Ryan, so reliable behind the plate, would do the catching, and Toms River could go with Austin, Andrew, Pauly, Johnny and Scotty around the infield in whatever combination John needed. Vinny, Mo, Quintin and Billy Sullivan were ready to play the outfield, as was Drew Fanara. The only loss was Clayton Kapp. Clayton's hand still ached from getting hit by the Brick pitcher in Game 2; he would spend the rest of the tournament outside the dugout and off the roster card, meaning Toms River would go with 12 players.

The Toms River players and coaches knew a little about the Manchester team. Without question, everyone knew who Aaron Kane was. Kane had been bombing his way through the tournament, driving homers out in almost every game he had played. He was a big kid who had gotten much bigger over the past year—"He looks like he ought to be playing for Holbrook," Vinny joked—and John was already trying to figure ways of neutralizing Kane's presence in the Manchester lineup. He figured Manchester would bat

Kane at the top of the order, to get him the most trips to the plate that they could—and Aaron was also going to be the starting pitcher. He was that good, a Scotty Ringel type. He was one of those kids who could do it all.

Manchester's only defeat in pool play had been to Jackson, and even that had been a great game, a 5–2 final score. In its other three games, Manchester had scored 34 runs and allowed only five. Johnny and Scotty had no trouble conjuring a healthy respect, especially when they remembered how close their games had been when they met Manchester in each of the last two district tourneys.

Coach Scott Ringel shared the sentiment. "These last two years, if you were to ask me, I'd say that any one of about seven or eight teams could have won the district. Basically, just about any team that got out of pool play could win. Manchester was certainly good enough to win. There's an awful lot of talent in this district. You look at the section results year by year, and the champ from District 18 is winning the section most of the time. It's getting out of here that's so hard."

And that was where Chris came in. John again had weighed his options on the mound, and he knew he had to decide between Chris and Johnny. Choosing Chris was actually the easy way out: If he got into trouble, Johnny could come in to pitch, and John felt that his son would throw strikes. If John flip-flopped the assignment and started Johnny, it meant that Chris would have to be rock solid when he came into the game in relief, because there were very few choices to pitch beyond those two. John couldn't be sure how Chris would respond to that pressure. And emotionally,

John knew that Chris felt comfortable starting games as the pitcher. Starting games was what Chris did.

John carried his optimism with him into the ballpark. In fact, he wasted no time that morning at the pre-game batting practice at Mapletree, telling the boys, "We'll win this one, we'll come back Wednesday and we'll win then." He was already trying to get the players to see their futures again, to get them excited about trying to run the table of the tournament. In his address to the kids, John made beating Manchester seem like a done deal.

It seemed odd coming right after a game like the one against Holbrook. Scotty already had decided that the game was meaningless in the big picture—but the *way* his team had lost bothered him deeply. It was as if only about half the guys had really come to play, and that felt like the continuation of a recent trend. In 2006, any team member might step up and carry the team, not just the stars. This year, if Scotty or Johnny or maybe Quintin didn't do it, it just might not get done, or at least that was how it seemed sometimes. Last summer it had been one cool hero after the next. If the Americans were going to get it together in 2007, they needed to start today.

In a twist of scheduling, the Holbrook team had been assigned the field right next to Toms River's field for its play-off game at the Berkeley complex. As Johnny looked over there, he could see Holbrook getting ready, and he could see its opponent, Brick National warming up on the other side. *That should be us playing Brick,* Johnny thought to himself. If his team hadn't imploded yesterday, it would be. But it was too late now; Johnny had to depend on hope. He had to hope Chris would be as good as he had been in the past. If Chris could put it together, Johnny thought, the Manchester guys would never know what hit them.

Out in the stands beyond the outfield fence, the mood among the Toms River families was slightly restrained. The parents joked about the day before, but only lightly. Individually, they felt that they'd done good jobs of keeping their children loose and reminding them that, after all, it was only one baseball game. But as Vinny's dad noted plainly, "That was a beating. It's hard to put one like that behind you." And he knew it was doubly hard for a defending champion from Toms River. The parents shared a certain amount of embarrassment with their sons. As a group, these parents had always been careful not to insult their kids by pretending the games were any less important than they actually felt. All relativism aside, the boys were into it. The *parents* were into it. As Pauly's mom, Lisa, sat in the stands over those first few games, the conversation about getting to Williamsport flowed freely; parents were asking questions about the drive to Pennsylvania and lodging and such. "We were all saying, 'Wouldn't that be great? Wouldn't it be so great?'" Lisa said. "We didn't mind talking about it because the boys were talking about it." The kids weren't the only ones who wanted to go for it. But having put their ambition out there, it would be the height of hypocrisy now for those same parents to turn around and try to downplay such a loss. Everyone knew how Toms River felt about Little League baseball. The parents, too, had been unnerved by the Holbrook debacle.

Taking a seat close to the Americans' dugout along first base, Donna Gulla felt the apprehension ratchet up inside her. Donna and Dennis both had seen Chris succeed in so many situations that they had moved past the point of being nervous on his behalf—they both felt that Chris would give everything he had—but Donna knew her son hadn't pitched much lately. This was a critical game—the only game, really, that could possibly matter now. That was the nerve-wracking part, the thought that it was Chris who needed to come through.

Donna had been a little surprised by John's choice to go with Chris. For weeks, the Gullas had worried that Chris's injuries were disappointing John. "John never would say anything like that, of course," Donna said, "but it was more just the fact that we really needed the pitching, and last year Chris had done so well. We didn't want to let John down." The Manchester game, in so many ways, was the first step on that long road back, and Donna knew that John was sending her son a message.

Chris wanted to succeed now, too, but for some reason he couldn't convince himself that he was ready. As he warmed up, Chris had trouble determining if he was on his game, in trouble or somewhere in between. It had been so long since he had thrown very much that even the warm-up pitches felt a little strange. His changeup was working well, and he wasn't having a problem putting his fastball where he wanted it. But that only put him halfway to where he needed to be.

Jerry Volk had seen enough of the Manchester players to know that they were solid, especially at the top of their batting order. There was no question that Manchester's kids were going to get their hits today; the question was how

Chris, and by extension the Americans as a team, would respond. For the first time in a long, long time, Jerry felt unsure. Even in the early pool-play games, when the boys had struggled and needed to come back to beat Berkeley and Brick, Jerry had remained confident that the team was going to be fine. But after the Holbrook game, Jerry began to reconsider the Americans' chances. He knew these kids so well; he had coached most of them for years. He had never seen them play so badly, fall apart so quickly, or respond so absently as they had against Holbrook.

And Jerry worried, too, that Chris was going to have a hard time. That was just the coach's sense of things. He didn't see the fire in Chris's eyes, and even though there weren't many options, Jerry's feeling was to want to put the ball in the glove of a player who couldn't wait to accept it. He might've just thrown Johnny out there for all the marbles, given the way Johnny had been competing so far in the tournament. But he knew John wasn't going to do it, and Jerry understood that. He just couldn't shake the feeling that the better pitcher, Johnny, was going to be playing shortstop instead of taking control of the game on the mound.

On Saturday night, with Holbrook in the past and Manchester coming up, Kelly Volk, the self-acknowledged worrier, asked her husband if things were going to be okay. Kelly made it a habit of asking Jerry that question when it came to Mo's games, because Jerry always seemed to have a reassuring reply at the ready. This time, Jerry said, "Well, I don't know," fell silent, and let it go at that.

John, too, had had a moment of doubt, and it took him aback. Driving home on Saturday after the Holbrook game, he wondered if the Americans' performance he had just seen was a harbinger of things to come. The magnitude of the defeat felt ominous enough. John privately loved the fact that Johnny had been so annoyed by the particulars of the defeat, but the coach also could see that some of the other kids simply looked bereft. They almost seemed bewildered by their collective inability to raise their game. It was a bad look for them, and for John.

So John had decided to go back to the basics, to the thoughts that made him optimistic and ready to come out and coach again. He had Chris Gulla on the mound against Manchester, and Chris was a big-game pitcher. Scotty would come up huge. Johnny would make some plays. Quintin surely had a great moment inside him. John always told the guys that he wouldn't trade them for any other Little Leaguers. They now had a great chance to reward that faith.

By noon in Berkeley Township, the sun had made its way near the top of the sky, and decent shade was but a rumor. The concession stand, which sat in the middle of three of the baseball fields at the Moorage Baseball Complex like the hub of a wheel, was doing killer business in Gatorade, water and soda. The weather reminded Anthony Schifilliti a little bit of last summer, when so many days turned from warm to oppressively hot, and the Toms River families responded by calling for a pool party or a pizza picnic after just about every game. Almost the entire team got together, every time. The Puleos alone must have hosted half a dozen times. It had been a summer of fast food, postgame swims, spur-of-the-moment sleepovers, and championship baseball. In other words, it had been just about perfect.

Now, the high sun meant that it was time to start the game—and Chris was going to be challenged right away. Manchester had indeed put Aaron Kane at the top of the batting order. Chris worked carefully, trying to nibble at the corners of home plate rather than put a pitch anywhere Kane could get a full swing on it. It was John's plan: he'd rather give up a walk to Kane than give up a huge hit. But Kane still got his bat on a fastball and sent it out to center field, and when the ball buzzed under Quintin's glove, Aaron made it to second base. Chris Gulla already was facing a test.

And just like that, Chris responded. After giving up a fly ball that allowed Kane to tag up and reach third base, Chris took a deep breath, stepped back on the pitching rubber and struck out the number-three hitter in the Manchester lineup, and then he got the third out on a fly to Vinny in right. An inning later, Chris walked out there and did it again, and this time he set down the Manchester batters one-two-three, a quick and efficient inning. His fastball appeared to be humming in there pretty well, and his changeup was moving and disrupting the Manchester hitters. From the dugout, John smiled to himself. It was early, but Chris looked for all the world like the player who helped carry this team to victory a year ago.

Chris, though, already was beginning to have his doubts. It had been a long time since he pitched more than an inning, and it had been a long time since he had been pitching in a game this important. In the dugout before the game against Holbrook on Saturday, the kids had still been talking about Williamsport, still fully believing that it was their destiny to get there. Now all of that talk had come to a halt, because their chances pretty much depended on what Chris could get done in this game, and nobody, not even Chris himself, was sure. His arm felt funny. It wasn't hurting, or at least not yet, but it didn't feel quite right, either. Chris was having a hard time identifying the problem, even though he seemed to be pitching well enough through two innings. He wasn't pitching the way he wanted to.

Still, John's concern in the first part of the game wasn't Chris; it was the Toms River hitters. They hadn't exactly been an explosive team in the tournament to this point, and now they were really struggling against Kane. They had a chance in the second inning, after Scotty worked the count to 2–2 and then hit a ground ball in between first and second base. The first baseman went to his right to knock down the ball, and Kane came hustling over from the mound to cover first base. Scotty got there at the same time as the throw. The ump called him out.

"He was safe," Scott Ringel said matter-of-factly. "But you don't always get that call."

It was a 0–0 score after two innings. John looked at his own lineup; they were flailing against Kane's pitches, really struggling to get a bat on the ball. The coach hoped that Chris had one of his classic pitching performances in him.

What John didn't see was that, in between innings, Chris was sitting in the dugout with an iced-down towel wrapped around his pitching arm. Chris had decided to do that on his own, after his dad had brought him a cooler with some drinks in it. He took the towel and put it in the ice inside the cooler, then came to the dugout after each inning and got out the towel and put it on the arm. In his own way, Chris was trying to stay one step ahead of the tendonitis, anticipating the pain that he thought would arrive, even though what he was doing actually made no sense. In general, what a pitcher needed to do was to keep the throwing arm warm, not cool; this was the reason why so many pitchers, young and old, wore jacket sleeves over their arms as they sat in the dugout. Icing the arm between innings would have the opposite effect, making the limb stiffer when the goal should be to keep it loose. Chris may not have been hurting himself, but he certainly wasn't doing the arm any good.

For Scott Ringel, though, the issue was that Chris was showing no signs of wanting to pitch. Scott was in the announcer's booth, directly behind home plate, to help with the scorekeeping. He had a great view. He could see in Chris's body language and his facial expressions that he wasn't sure of himself. Scott felt that John was going to have to make a pitching move before this game got too far along.

Scott didn't argue with the logic of starting Chris, but he favored a quick hook. He had complete sympathy for what Chris had gone through during the spring; he understood where Chris was coming from. But the baseball field, in the middle of an elimination game, wasn't the time or place to sort it all out. Toms River needed a win.

In the top of the third inning, Chris gave up a leadoff single to the Manchester catcher, and the following batter hit a ball down the first-base line that Austin, moving to his left, couldn't control. The ball skittered out to right field. Vinny fielded it and came up throwing, but the runner slid into second base under the tag—another close call—and now there were runners at second and third with no outs. The batter was Aaron Kane.

Now John Puleo, sending signs to Ryan from the dugout, knew what he wanted to do—and he knew that it was a risk. He ordered Kane to be walked intentionally, which under the new Little League rules meant that Chris didn't even have to throw the four balls. The team merely had to inform the umpire that Kane was to be awarded first base.

The move unnerved Chris. He had never been told to intentionally walk anybody. It felt like a concession, which added to Chris's general sense that he was struggling. Toms River had just allowed another Manchester kid to reach first, and now the bases were loaded because of it.

But John knew it was the right call, risk or no risk. By loading the bases, he had put Chris in a position where his infielders could record a force-out at any base. They could throw home on a ground ball and get an out without allowing a run to score or even needing to apply a risky tag. And, more to the point, the walk meant that Aaron Kane couldn't launch a game-changing blast. This was really the only practical thing to do.

John believed that Chris could get the other hitters out. Kane was the real problem. John felt that Chris could use his changeup and the location on his fastball to navigate the danger zones with the other guys. Emotionally, though, Chris was working without a net. Jerry could see it just as Scott saw it. Between batters, Chris's eyes would glance into the dugout, as if he were waiting for John to come and take him out of the game. When he got two quick strikes on

Eddie White, the batter who followed Kane in the lineup, Chris suddenly bounced a pitch to the backstop. Only a good ricochet and Ryan's quick footwork prevented the runner at third from trying to score. One pitch later, White drove a ball into right field, and when Vinny left his feet to make a diving catch, the runner at third tagged up and scored. Manchester had drawn first blood. It was 1–0.

It was only one run. But Chris already was beginning to feel like a car running on its last fumes of gas. With one out, he managed to record a strikeout with a great changeup, but the next batter smashed a wicked line drive up the middle. This time, Johnny bailed Chris out with an acrobatic play, diving to his left from his shortstop position and snaring the liner for the final out of the inning. Johnny ran off the field to the back-slapping congratulations of his teammates, and he knew he'd just saved at least one run, maybe two. He also knew that he was about to pitch. Johnny was sure of that, and he was ready. He had been great two games ago. He felt strong. Surely his dad would be calling on him next, because Chris was done. Anybody could see that.

Only Chris wasn't done. He still had a couple of surprises left. And the first one arrived with a bat in his hand.

With Kane still pitching for Manchester, Austin drew a walk to lead off the bottom of the third. The next batter was Chris, and the boy who strode up to home plate was not the same person who had just been pitching. There was a reason for that: Even through the worst of his arm trouble, Chris had been able to swing the bat. It was the one thing that never seemed to cause him pain. He hadn't forgotten how to hit. He wasn't a big guy, but, like Johnny, he knew that serious hitting was about timing and bat speed, not necessarily raw strength. He was a contact hitter. He knew the sound his bat made when he hit something square. And though he projected almost no confidence as a pitcher right now, he was a different creature with that batting helmet on.

It was a 2–2 pitch that cost Aaron Kane the lead. Chris barely felt the ball hit his bat. It was a sweet-spot hit, and the ball jumped. It had barely begun to climb into the air when, in the stands, Austin Higgins's father, Doug, got on his feet and began applauding, because Doug knew where the thing was going: on a straight line over the center-field fence.

The thing about Little League was that games often changed completely in an instant such as this. One swing from a skilled player could alter the course of events. John had believed all along that he needed Chris in the game, and now he realized why. Toms River had a 2–1 lead—and Aaron Kane, for the first time, blinked.

The next batter was Andrew, and when he ripped a double down the right-field line, the Americans started to think they were going to take the great Kane down. With one out and Quintin at the plate, Andrew stole third, and now all Q had to do was put the ball in play somewhere to get Andrew home. This was the kind of pressure situation that Quintin lived for. But Kane was up for a battle, too. After working the count to 3–1, Quintin fouled off three straight pitches, with Kane refusing to give in and walk him. It was a great sequence, Kane blasting fastballs in there and Quintin fouling them back. On the next pitch, Kane reached back and threw his hardest fastball yet. Quintin saw the pitch and went for it, but he was one millisecond slow. He swung and missed for strike three, the Manchester fans coming to their feet to roar their approval. When Scotty subsequently grounded out to first on another close call, the rally died.

The sequence seemed to take the wind out of the Toms River kids. Kane had looked so vulnerable; he was just one good hit away from being chased off the pitcher's mound. Quintin was the guy to deliver that hit, but he hadn't been able to get it done. He actually had a good at-bat, making Kane work on every pitch. But the name of the game in that situation was contact—a grounder, a deep fly ball, anything but a strikeout.

It was an exchange of emotion: Kane had been the one who gave up the two-run homer, yet it was his Manchester team that ran off the field excitedly. Kane, to use the old baseball phrase, had dodged a bullet. The chance to knock him out had been there. Toms River now had the lead but not the momentum.

LOOKING BACK, THERE WERE THREE decisions at Berkeley on July 8 that defined the summer of hope for the Toms River Americans, and two of them directly involved Chris Gulla. The first was the decision by John to start Chris on the mound. The second was the one to keep him there.

From her spot in the stands, Diane Puleo looked on in some amazement as she saw Chris walk out toward the pitcher's mound to begin the fourth inning. Diane had just assumed, along with most of the Toms River parents, that it would be her son Johnny coming in to protect the 2–1 lead and get the Americans to the next round. From her vantage point, Chris had looked finished after the third inning. In the bleachers around her, she heard a parent ask, "Chris is going again?" And, almost reflexively, she picked up her cell phone and began to key in the numbers to call John.

Deep down, she knew John wouldn't answer, but Diane was a competitor, too. As difficult as it might be for her to watch Johnny shoulder the weight of the game, she felt that putting her son on the mound was the right thing to do. All in all, Chris had done an amazing job to get Toms River to where it was. Heck, it was his home run that had the team ahead. This was the perfect time to move.

Scott Ringel thought so. Jerry Volk thought so. Donna Gulla didn't need to see anything more; she could tell that Chris had already given whatever he had to give. But John wanted one more inning. He hadn't thought much beyond that. What he saw was that Chris had wobbled slightly in the third, then been saved by Johnny's great play at shortstop on the line drive. If Johnny were pitching and someone else playing short, would that same defensive stop have been made? And in John's mind, Johnny's play had given Chris the only escape he would need. Pitchers did that all the time, getting the benefit of a solid defensive effort that helped them right themselves and start throwing great again.

And when you put it all in the big picture, Chris was ahead 2–1 in the fourth inning of a District 18 playoff game. You could argue that he was out-pitching Kane. John wasn't focusing on the balls that had been hit hard off Chris; he was focusing on the idea that Chris could get him three more outs, because Chris would be facing the bottom of the Manchester batting order. That would set up Johnny to come in for the fifth inning to face the top of the order, and give Aaron Kane a new pitcher to contend with.

John's plan smacked of positive thoughts. He was gearing his ideas toward the best that could happen, not the worst. The problem was, Chris really was done. And John was the only one who didn't see it.

THREE PITCHES INTO THE FOURTH inning, the game was tied 2–2. Chris delivered a fastball that a Manchester batter hit so hard it ricocheted off the scoreboard beyond left field. In the field, Johnny mentally prepared to begin pitching. In the stands, Diane again punched the numbers on her cell phone. Behind home plate, Scott saw Chris look into the dugout, waiting for John to come get him. But John held fast. A solo home run in Little League was something that happened all the time. He wasn't going to panic over it. He wanted Chris to get through the inning, and he believed Chris could do it.

And out there in the hot afternoon sun, Chris Gulla tried. He struck out the next batter he faced. He struck out the one after that. It was a 2–2 game with two outs in the fourth, and when he got two quick strikes on the Manchester catcher it looked as if the inning was over.

But Chris was reaching his limit—physically, emotionally, all of it. "When you looked in Chris's eyes, it was a big game and he didn't know how to handle it," Scott Ringel said. "He kept looking in the dugout, like, 'Take me out.' You know, they're kids. You can't blame kids. Some of them want the ball at the end of the game, and some of them don't. And that can change from year to year. Or week to week."

Here, now, in the fourth inning, Chris was beginning to look like a kid again. With the count 0–2 on the catcher, Chris suddenly lost his focus completely. He threw four straight balls, the fourth one hitting the batter on the foot. He walked the next batter on four straight pitches. That quickly, Manchester had runners at first and second, and the bottom of the order was finished batting. The next player up was Aaron Kane.

John faced another quick decision. He knew that Johnny was ready to pitch, and under his original strategy, Johnny likely would have faced Kane to begin the fifth inning anyway. But that would be a situation with the bases empty. Here there were two runners on base, and John didn't want to bring his son into that kind of pressure situation.

So he made a two-pronged decision: He would keep Chris on the mound, and he would take the bat out of Kane's hands. John again ordered Chris to walk Kane on purpose.

From his spot in the outfield, Vinny couldn't believe what he was seeing. The first time his team had intentionally walked Kane, first base had been open. The strategy made sense because it set up force plays all over the field. This time, the runners were only on first and second base. The walk would actually be moving the runners ahead one base. It was a rare baseball move to walk a batter to a base that was already occupied. Vinny blanched at the thought. He'd have rather seen Toms River—his team—just go right after Kane. Play baseball. Make him swing the bat.

Pauly felt the same way, and Scotty, too—they just

couldn't understand it. Coach John usually played for the win, played to the aggressive side, the positive side. Now he seemed to be trying to avoid the worst. From where they stood, if John was trying to limit the damage he would pull Chris and replace him with Johnny. Yet their coach hadn't made that move.

In fact, John didn't visit Chris at all. He didn't go out there after the home run, even as Donna waited expectantly for that to happen. She figured John to ask her son, "Are you ready to come out?" or to tell him to keep going.

Chris, too, was waiting for a mound conference that didn't happen. When he lost the plate after being ahead 0–2 with two outs, Chris actually found himself turning fully toward the dugout and looking in.

"I was looking at him, like wondering if he was going to take me out," Chris said. "I kind of wanted him to. I wanted to pitch, but I didn't want to ruin the game."

But John had made up his mind. Chris was going to get out of the jam, and Toms River would take a 2–2 tie into the bottom of the fourth inning, and Johnny would come in and slam the door shut on the Manchester hitters. Kane grudgingly took his intentional walk, a frown on his face, and the runners moved up. The bases were loaded with two out.

WHEN EDDIE WHITE HIT CHRIS'S high inside fastball, it felt like time stopped. The ball was just struck so magnificently; it was the cleanest hit you ever saw. The way it shot off the bat—the DeMarini composite model that didn't make a pinging sound at contact but rather a duller, more muted thunk—just left no doubt. Chris didn't need to look; he could tell from Ryan's expression behind the plate that the ball had sprouted wings. It was up over everybody's head before you blinked. John came out from the dugout and squinted into the bright sun, trying to see where the ball was going. It was going and going. It landed on the roof of the concession stand, the building that sat between the three fields at Moorage and way, way beyond the outfield fence. Vinny actually found himself smiling a little, not because he was happy about anything but because he'd never actually seen a ball hit that far, or that hard.

"I just watched it go," Vinny said. "It was a bomb. All I saw was—boom."

Johnny watched it. Scotty did, for a second. Chris never did look up. Like the other guys, he had played in plenty of baseball games. He didn't need to see the ball land to know Toms River was in trouble.

Eddie White circled the bases fairly quickly, all things considered. He kept his head down. Johnny recognized the stride and the look: Eddie wore the same expressionless mask that Johnny donned most of the time when he played. Only when Eddie crossed home plate, to be mobbed and pounded on the back by his teammates, did it become obvious what a huge thing he had done. Only then did John Puleo begin to calculate the damage.

It took a while to add up.

THE AFTERNOON WAS A BLUR, a swirl of colors and humidity, of the cheering Manchester crowd, the vision of Eddie White's ball bouncing off the roof of the concession stand. When it was over, a few stark images lingered in the mind.

One was the sight of Johnny Puleo on the pitcher's mound in the fifth and sixth innings, virtually and unmistakably unhittable. Johnny retired all six batters he faced, striking out the side in the top of the sixth. He struck out Aaron Kane. For the tournament, he allowed one hit in almost seven innings of work. That made him Toms River's most effective pitcher of the summer.

There was the image of John getting in his players' faces before the bottom of the fourth, after Eddie White's home run, exhorting the boys to continue playing hard, not to allow one blow to knock them down.

"I don't want to see anybody hanging his head!" John barked. "I want to see fight! I want to see guts! I want to see heart! I want to see one thing: The same thing we had against Jackson last year. Remember Jackson!"

The Toms River hitters went out down in order, and the fourth inning was over.

There was Quintin in the batter's box, with runners on first and second and two outs in the fifth inning. Aaron Kane had been pulled from the mound, a relief pitcher in his place. Q went up with another chance to change the course of the game. He saw four pitches. The fourth was a called strike three, with Quintin left standing there looking, the bat never having left his shoulder. It was a great pitch, off-speed. Quintin bent over, holding his helmet in both hands, his face the contorted picture of agony. Around him, the Manchester kids ran to their dugout, laughing, chatting, sure now that the game was theirs to win. At the third-base coach's box, John stood there and watched Q for a moment. The image broke John's heart.

There was, finally, a hint of a rally in the bottom of the sixth—and wasn't that what Coach John always wanted, six good innings? Scotty singled, and Johnny hit a shot to the fence that scored him, and the Manchester kids started to tighten a little in the field. Drew hit a bloop that landed behind the pitcher's mound, but nobody converged on it, and Drew was safe at first. The score was 6–3, and Toms River had runners at first and second with nobody out.

"It's your time!" Kim Sullivan called from the stands. "Come on, guys, it's your time!"

Ryan was the next batter, and with two strikes he managed to foul off two pitches and stay alive. Finally, he got just enough of his bat on the ball to hit a grounder between shortstop and third base. Both fielders moved over to cover it, but the ball somehow trickled through and rolled out to left field.

"Go! Go!" John shouted to Johnny, who had been held up between second and third waiting to see if the ball would get through. Now Johnny reached third and, hearing his dad and seeing John's windmill arm motion, obediently took off for home and scored. But at second base, Drew thought John's command was for him, and he continued past the bag, steaming toward third. The Manchester outfielder, looking up, was shocked to see Drew on the move. He threw an easy strike to the base. Drew was out.

Toms River had only one out and had pulled to within 6–4—yet for the second time in the game, it felt as though Manchester had won the play. The out at third seemed to calm the Manchester players a little, at the same time that it silenced the roaring Toms River crowd. The Toms River fans couldn't believe Drew had been thrown out. It was a simple mistake. John had intended his words and gestures for Johnny. He didn't realize that Drew was going off those same signals.

"We should *still* be playing that inning," John would say, two months after the game.

Pauly tried to get the rally started up again, but instead chased a high inside pitch and struck out. The Americans were down to their final out, needing a two-run homer to tie the game, keep the dream going. The batter was Chris Gulla.

And that image lingered, too, that last image of the season. With the game still in doubt, Chris took a ball high, then another pitch low. He fouled off the next offering, making the count 2–1. He could still expect a strike—and he got one. But Chris had already enjoyed his home-run moment for the day; this time he swung late at the pitch and hit a sharp grounder to the first baseman.

With the game on the line, though, the first baseman fumbled the ball, and it kicked away from him to his right. Chris's heart leaped: He still had a chance at being safe. The noise from the crowd was incredible; you couldn't hear anything but the screams of the parents on both sides of the field. The boy at first scrambled frantically after the ball, then retreated to his bag in hopes of taking a throw. Chris tore his way up the first-base line. The second baseman sprinted to his left to get the ball, and he got a clean handle on it and got ready to toss the ball to first. It was going to be close.

And in that instant, Chris became a kid again, just a kid playing a game. Inexplicably, he chose to dive the last couple of feet to first base. Diving head-first toward any base in Little League constituted an automatic out under the rules, but it didn't matter: the throw beat Chris anyway. The second baseman had come up with the ball just in time. He really made a fine play, and, at the time, a fine play was needed to win the game.

The Manchester kids stormed toward one another, jumping up and down in celebration. This was no ordinary victory; they had just taken out the defending District 18 champion. They weren't going to have to listen to the Toms River talk this summer. They had just taken care of that.

In the Toms River dugout, there was a stony silence. The quiet was briefly penetrated by Johnny, who wordlessly slammed some equipment against the fence. Otherwise there was no sound other than the sniffling of a few teary-eyed boys. Scotty stood up and got ready to go; he couldn't see the point of lingering over the defeat. Chris walked slowly off the infield, the dust of the game's final play still caked on his jersey. At one end of the bench, Quintin sat and stared across the field. He felt empty. Pauly sat with him for a few moments, a friend beside a friend. Then, lacking any better ideas, Pauly began to pack his gear one final time.

It was only July.

For the first time in a long time, John wasn't sure how to act. He felt sick to his stomach, on the verge of tears himself. As proper a perspective as he felt he had on Little League, the truth was that John had wanted to go to Williamsport as much as any of the players. In some ways, he wanted it more than they did; after all, he was carrying their hopes along with his own every time he coached.

John walked to the dugout and called the boys together to go shake hands with the Manchester team. It was tradition. Pauly went through the line with his head down, not making eye contact with the Manchester guys. As he passed, he heard one of them whisper, "Big girls don't cry."

John began putting the bats and helmets in the team equipment bag. He was aware that the families were massing just outside the dugout. It was hard to believe that he found himself trying to come up with some sort of consolation to offer them and their sons. The dream died so hard around here.

"Here, everybody get close," John finally said. "I want to talk to the boys."

When the boys were all there, John spent a minute reminding them of the summer of 2006, not to pour salt in the wound, but to rekindle the pride they had felt winning those championships for Toms River Little League. When the summer ended that year, the league hung two banners inside its indoor training facility, one each for the district and section championship.

"Remember those banners, because they're never coming down," John told the boys now. "No one can take those away from you. We did that together, and I wouldn't trade you for any group of players in the world. It didn't go our way today. Some days are like that. You've got nothing to be ashamed of."

With that, John fell silent, and the boys came in just a little closer. One of them called out for a parting cheer—"Toms River on three! Toms River on three! One, two three—Toms River!"—but it was a halfhearted effort. When someone asked Johnny what his father had told the kids,

Johnny replied with a thin smile, "I don't know. I wasn't listening."

He wasn't listening, maybe, because there was nothing he or his teammates could do now. The boys finished packing up their gear. Their parents fished for car keys in purses and pockets. It was still early afternoon, Sunday along the Jersey Shore.

The boys walked with their folks out to their cars. From across the street and down the block, a few of the guys exchanged waves. You could hear the sound of 10 or 11 car engines firing up at the same time. And for the first time in a long, long time, the Toms River Americans simply drove away.

EPILOGUE

IN LATE AUGUST OF 2007, on a field at Williamsport, Pennsylvania, that a week's worth of rain and baseball games had made sodden, a braces-wearing 12-year-old from Warner Robins, Georgia, struck one of the more dramatic home runs in recent memory. Dalton Carriker's hit, which sailed over the right-field fence, gave the Georgia team a 3–2, extra-innings victory over Japan, thus delivering the United States its third consecutive championship at the Little League World Series. Carriker, who had asked God to give him the strength "to get a hit and help my team out," was seen on worldwide television deliriously circling the bases; later, he said he couldn't even feel his legs as he ran. His face was the epitome of a kid's joy.

From a table at a restaurant just outside of Cooperstown, New York, Chris Gulla and his Toms River teammates watched the sequence play out on a big-screen TV. As they joked with each other, ate some pizza and followed the action inning by inning, the kids split almost down the middle on who to root for: half went for Japan, the other half for the United States. It was more fun that way, to have a little razzing back and forth. Taking a paper napkin out of the holder and wrapping it around his forehead, Chris reached for the ketchup bottle and dabbed a dot of red in the middle of the napkin, the better to resemble some of the Japan fans whose constant chants and cheers and waving Japanese flags were being shown on ABC. The World Series game was grand entertainment, a television programmer's dream. The nip-and-tuck contest featured lots of close-up camera shots of the kids in the field, their brows furrowed in concentration, and of their overwrought parents in the stands. Williamsport was the biggest stage.

Sitting a little farther down the table, Johnny Puleo watched the game with interest. He measured the players from Georgia and Japan against his Toms River Americans—how hard the pitchers were throwing, the quality of the line drives and homers being hit, the defensive plays—and as he did so he became more and more convinced of the quality of his own team.

"We could beat 'em," Johnny finally declared. "We could, if we played well. They're not that great, actually."

Johnny couldn't prove it, but he didn't need to. For him, having the thought to hold on to was enough.

It was Coach John's idea to come to Cooperstown. In fact, he had entered his Bengals team, basically the Little League All-Star roster by another name, in the August Cooperstown Tournament long before the Toms River Americans' World Series dreams died in July in Berkeley Township. The tournament was a weeklong schedule of games that brought travel teams from all across the country to one destination, where they stayed in dormitory-style housing and tried to battle their way through a field of 96 entries. The format was a sort of ultimate-fighter-style process, and it was ruthlessly efficient. Each team played a bunch of games to get their money's worth, and after those compulsories, the main event began: a single-elimination sprint to the finish. If you lost a game, you packed up and went home.

The Cooperstown complex put one of these tournaments together every week, all summer long, drawing many of the elite youth baseball programs in the United States. Some were year-round travel squads, who drafted players from different regions onto a single roster; some even pulled in players from several states to play together. These were teams that existed solely to win games and tournaments, collections of stars who were usually the best individual players in each of the areas where they lived. Those kids—and their coaches—generally dismissed Little League as a quaint, town-team approach to the game, and even a Little League World Series champion roster would be no match for some of the rolling supersquads that came through here.

John had signed up his Bengals team knowing full well they were a local collection of talent, a bunch of guys from the same zip code. They were in Cooperstown to have fun more than to compete seriously for a championship. As he originally conceived it, John thought of the tourney as a reward, a great way to end a long, wearing summer of baseball. He had been anticipating another All-Star season of 56 straight days of Little League—or more, depending on how far the Toms River Americans went. John chose the end of August for the Cooperstown tourney, in fact, to minimize the conflict with an extended Little League playoff run.

After the Manchester game, John wanted the kids back on the ball field as soon as possible. He wanted the District 18 tournament to become a memory. He felt a need to get the boys—and their parents—thinking about the future again. For John, heading back into baseball games was the only acceptable antidote to the Americans' Little League finish. The ending had been so abrupt and so painful that he couldn't imagine allowing it to stand as the only memory of the summer. For that matter, he didn't even want to give it time to sink in with the kids. After all the talk about going to the World Series, the best thing now was to get it behind them and move on. Even with football and soccer encroaching on their time, the Bengals were planning to play a full schedule through the fall.

"You've got to get them back out there, playing ball," John said. "You need them back on the field, having fun, doing the stuff they do—telling their jokes and taking batting practice and all that. I mean, it's baseball."

John paused for a moment, thinking. "You know, the dream died. It died. But there's always a new dream. When you're twelve? Come on—there's always a new dream."

THE REST OF THE LITTLE League District 18 All-Star tournament played out about as John expected. With Toms River American out of the way, the path to the finals was clear for the two best remaining teams, Jackson and Holbrook. Jackson reached the title game by scoring a 9–4 victory over Manchester in the semis; spectators could see that Aaron Kane and his Manchester teammates had used most of their emotional reserve in the huge win over the Americans. Holbrook, meanwhile, came into the championship game on a roll, having scored 25 runs in its last two games—43 in three games, if you counted the Toms River slaughter at the end of pool play.

On a muggy Jersey Shore evening on July 14, the District 18 championship set up as a great showdown between two neighboring Little Leagues. Jackson, though, had the superior pitching, and for first time all summer, the Holbrook bats fell silent. Jackson's All-Stars won the game 9–1 to cap a brilliant tournament; they allowed only eight total runs in seven games. The players fell into a dog pile near the pitcher's mound, then gleefully posed for photos while holding their new championship banner. The celebration occurred on the Toms River Americans' home field, Scavuzzo, which had been chosen to host the title game.

As so often had happened over the years, the district champ from the Toms River's area was also the best team in the section. Jackson steamed through that competition, and went on to the state tournament in Clayton, where it reached the finals before losing. Tracking the results over those last couple of weeks in July, John imagined that his Americans could have traveled the same path. They just couldn't get out of their own district.

As it developed, though, John's was not the last Toms River squad standing that summer. That distinction went to a team from Toms River East Little League, coached by John Cardini, another longtime presence on the local scene. Cardini's team, TRELL National, got out of its pool play with a 3–1 record and then defeated Toms River National 6–1 in the quarterfinals, a game played on the field in Holbrook roughly 24 hours after Puleo's team had been destroyed there—and at about the same time that the Americans were being eliminated by Manchester a few townships over.

Cardini was a plainspoken and unapologetically competitive man whose daughter was an All-Star, and he had no illusions about the level of expectation on him or his team. Once upon a time, after all, his league had produced three World Series qualifiers in five years, and although TRELL hadn't made a serious run at Williamsport since Mike Gaynor's last team in 1999, the league-wide desire to repeat the performance had not waned. When someone congratulated him on beating Toms River National, Cardini chuckled and replied, "Nobody gets high-fived around here for winning the first round."

A few days later, Holbrook took Cardini's team out of the tournament in the semifinals. The game was close at the start—3–1 in the second inning. But rain forced a postponement, and play did not resume until the following day. When the game finally began again, TRELL just didn't look the same, and Holbrook's hitters brought out their whipping sticks. The final score was 13–3. If the rain hadn't come, maybe things would have gone differently. As it was, for the eighth straight year, the Toms River community's hopes for a World Series appearance were dashed.

WHEN HE TRIED TO PARSE the meaning of what had happened to his team, John Puleo found himself surrounded by doubt. He couldn't help it. He walked off the field in

Berkeley and into an extended period of self-examination, constantly rewinding the sequence of the last few games in his mind and second-guessing the decisions he had made along the way.

He could see easily where the competitive thread had unraveled: using Scotty for a few too many pitches against Toms River National had screwed up the rotation plans for the playoffs, and once the pitching lineup was off-kilter, everything felt like a struggle. But that was too simple an answer. John looked deeper. Had he really done everything he could on behalf of the kids?

He wondered about his practices. Had they been too tough, or not tough enough? He wondered about the Holbrook game, when Pauly was pitching well. Should he have left Pauly in there for another inning or two? And the Manchester game, the one that sealed his team's fate—what had gone wrong there? Were his thoughts scattered that day? Shouldn't he have put Johnny in sooner to pitch, when Chris clearly was struggling? Had he held off using Johnny as pitcher simply because he didn't want to risk seeing his son fail?

Taken individually, the questions that John asked himself were all valid; it isn't as though Little League coaches were immune from second-guessing because they happened to work with children rather than high school, college or pro players. But John was forgetting the larger picture, which was that what the Toms River teams tried to accomplish every summer was, statistically speaking, the most improbable thing in the world. Reaching the Little League World Series, even with a great team, was very much akin to hitting the lottery; in addition to elite skill, a team needed to catch every break along the way. What Mike Gaynor's hard-working, fun-loving teams achieved at the end of the 1990s was a magnificent, brilliant, thrill-ride of a fluke—but nevertheless a fluke. There was a reason why so few Little Leagues ever made a repeat appearance in Williamsport.

"The boys went to the state tournament last year, and this year the thinking was, 'How do I do better?' And that's tough, it really is," said Donna Gulla. "It's pretty hard to top last year."

John was only marginally consoled by the stark truths of the summer of 2007, the ones that suggested what happened was more reasonable than not. For instance, playing three games in three days at the Little League level was brutally difficult under any circumstances, much less under the new pitch-count rules. But John was dogged by questions of what he could have done differently; they stayed with him even after summer ended. He took them into the fall, found himself often drifting back to the strategies and moves he'd made in the games. He never lost his positive train of thought, but he still turned the events of the summer over and over again in his mind.

On an October night, months after the Little League had ended, with Diane and his three children home with him to celebrate his 49th birthday, John suddenly leaned forward in his kitchen chair. Another baseball thought had struck him.

"They were too tight. I didn't do a good enough job of keeping them loose," John said. "We were supposed to stay loose and have fun, and I didn't do a good job with that."

"Come on!" Diane interjected. "You did everything you could. You blasted the music at practice, played hitting games at the end of the day—you did everything you could."

"I did the best I could, I guess," John said. "But in retrospect I don't think I did a good enough job of preparing them for adversity as I did when they were eleven. We were looser then."

Johnny, walking by the kitchen, overheard the exchange and stopped to listen a minute.

"Yeah, we were looser last year," he said.

"You were, right?" John said.

"Of course," Johnny replied matter-of-factly. "We didn't have the pressure to make it to Williamsport."

He said it with the slightest sense of relief. The World Series would be somebody else's problem next year. Johnny was going back to just playing ball.

IN THE LATE AFTERNOON OF July 8, 2007, the unmistakable sounds of a swim party emanated from the backyard of the home of John and Diane Puleo. Walking around the corner of the house, you could see Vinny about to cannonball his way into the pool; Johnny and Quintin, next in line on the diving board, were teasing and arguing about who could kick up the biggest splash. Up on the redwood deck, the tables were littered with pizza boxes and drinks.

John and Diane had seen the Toms River American All-Star team's season come to a close a few hours earlier, seen the families scatter so quickly from Berkeley Township. The summer before, pool parties were a regular way of life. They couldn't let this season end on such a comparatively solemn note.

So after stopping at their homes to change clothes, the Americans and their families met up at the Puleo place. John and Diane figured the boys would have a hard time feeling sorry for themselves while they were in the water. While the boys tried to goad Austin Higgins's dad into getting on the board for one of his record-setting, big-splash dives, John and Jerry Volk stood on the deck, sipping their drinks, talking things over. They still liked their team. John, in fact, was already warning the families that Bengals practice was going to begin in a week or two—"Get ready for more baseball!" he said jubilantly, drawing a laugh.

"Lots more fun to have," John said. "Let's get set for Cooperstown!"

This great, optimistic front was the side of John that most appealed to the parents. It was the reason that every family chose to continue on with John and the Bengals. At the end of the day, he was precisely the kind of adult with whom they wanted their children spending time. He was the role model.

In all the years he had coached her son, Kelly Volk couldn't remember John ever yelling at a player. "But I remember a batting practice before the Toms River National game this summer," she said. "He gave this, I don't know what you'd call it—the Iraq speech. There were a couple of kids around the batting cage who were kicking their stuff, throwing their equipment because they weren't hitting well, and John just had enough of that. He told them that there were men over in Iraq dying for our country so that the kids could wear that red, white and blue that they had on their uniforms—and he didn't want to hear the whining. He said it just like that. You didn't hear a sound from those kids."

Kelly smiled at the memory. "But even then, John kind of turned to us parents afterward and had this expression on his face, kind of winking at us. He had this big smile. He loved it. He didn't want to hear a bunch of whiners, that's all. Just hit the ball."

And this group of boys would continue to hit the ball, because the games would never end. There was Junior League baseball next spring, then Senior League, and then it was on to the high school programs, with their ultra-competitive tryouts and their top-10 statewide rankings. No one on John's team would shy away from that pressure. They were used to it. They had shouldered it already.

Down at poolside, John watched his younger son Matty goofing around with the older boys, trying to catch a tennis ball while airborne after leaving the diving board. The next evening, Matt's 10-year-old All-Star team would begin its own District 18 tournament, and John thought they had a chance to go deep. John knew most of Matt's teammates; he had just recently formed a Bengals II team in their age group to ensure that they would be able to play some travel-ball tournaments in the late summer and fall, so most of them already were playing for Coach John. In two years, when Matt was 12, he might get to be part of an All-Star team capable of dreaming its own big dream. John would enjoy that.

For the Americans, many of the kids had yet to process their loss to Manchester. Scotty Ringel took a silent ride home with his dad, crossing into his house before finally shaking his head and saying simply, "Not enough kids came to play this year." Pauly, who later said he felt "like we failed everyone," would spend the next month in such a funk, barely speaking to anyone, that his parents worried he might actually be sick.

Healing would take time; if the adults couldn't get over it

in one day, the boys couldn't, either. It would be weeks, in fact, before Johnny, lying on his bed one evening, would bolt upright, seemingly out of nowhere, and finally vent his emotion over the way All-Stars had gone. "We shouldn't have lost!" he would say to Diane, tears of frustration streaking down his cheeks as she rubbed his back and stroked his hair. "We could have won! We should never have lost that game!"

But the more he thought about it, the more John realized that the boys would be fine. The parents might struggle, he would struggle, but the boys would move on. John was sure of it that very day, standing on the deck of his house.

It was no mystery, after all. He could see it in front of him.

There, scattered around the lawn, were the boys of Toms River American, still in their swimsuits, dripping wet. They had abandoned the pool, left the folks all sitting in the backyard. Someone had found a Wiffle ball and bat, and the game was on; and when Johnny got a hold of one of Quintin's pitches and sent it soaring over the fence, the whole group of them took off toward the neighbor's gate, trash-talking and laughing, shoving one another out of the way, seeing who could be first to jump in the pool next door and retrieve the home-run ball.

You could hear the splashes, one after the other, and through the slats of the fence you could see the figures thrashing around, getting the ball out of the pool. The gate creaked as the boys came spilling back out, headed for the lawn. Someone held the yellow ball aloft, ready to pitch. The sooner they got back in play, the sooner they could resume the fun. The boys were ready.

ACKNOWLEDGMENTS

David Hirshey, resident bigwig at HarperCollins, is now 2-for–2 in hearing my ideas for books, resisting the temptation to dismiss them as either unrealistic or (possibly) substance-induced, and proceeding to clear the road for me to drive through with project in tow. I am happily indebted to him for his guidance, consistent encouragement and general good cheer. For a soccer fan, he appears sane, but then I don't see him regularly.

Kate Hamill edited this book with a wisdom beyond my years and a patience born, alas, of necessity. Without her willingness to do the heavy lifting, the resulting product would have been a substantially lesser thing, and her grace under pressure of deadline was remarkable. Any remaining lapses are my own, although if I can find someone to blame for them, I certainly will.

Bob Mecoy, at Creative Book Services, shepherded *Six Good Innings* from embryonic idea ("What about this town that always wins in Little League?") to finished product. His friendship and support are no less important than his ear for storytelling and his indispensable ability to wrangle money from publishers.

While I appreciate all those who gave their time and voices to the book, a specific thank-you is due one family. To John, Diane, Johnny, Matt and Sophia Puleo: Your willingness to open your home and your hearts was a tremendous gift, for which I am very grateful.

In New Jersey: Mike Gaynor, Joe Cudia, Scott Ringel, Vinny Ignatowicz, Doug Higgins, Jerry Volk, Kelly Volk, Donna Gulla, Ken Frank, Paul Fabricatore, John Cardini, Tom Hourigan, Anthony and Lisa Schifilliti, Jack Daubert, Charlie Frazier, Chris Cerullo, the boys of Toms River American Little League.

In Pennsylvania: Chris Downs, Little League International.

For perspective, food, drink and spiritual assistance unwittingly supplied: Michael "Duke" McIntyre, Andrea Boyles, Cameron and Kim Beck, the Borschel and LeClere families, Brian Brown, Michael and Donna Bass, Jim, Mitch, Kevin and Blake, the Hatamiya family, the James family. Love to Kay; my mother, Rachel; Don and Shelly; Johnny; Bob; Annette; Fitz; and to Kreidlers, Costellos, Woods, Janssens and FitzSimonses scattered about the globe.

My sons, Patric and Ryan, with their persistent love of baseball and baffling command of its minutiae, inspired the idea for this book while watching the Little League World Series nonstop several years ago during a vacation at the Sea Ranch, a community perched along the bluffs of the rugged and beautiful Northern California coast. Way to take in the scenery.

Without my wife, Colleen, my life would have followed a very different path indeed. She has provided the light and the space for two books and a dramatically redesigned way of living, and she has stood fast in hard times. My debt to her is obviously greater than I can repay—but I'll try.

Finally, sincere thanks to Steve Kreidler, who, eons ago, generously and repeatedly threw the kind of Wiffle ball pitches that he knew his little brother would be able to hit onto the home-run roof at the far end of the yard.